WORDS AND WANDERINGS

First published in 2010 by

WOODFIELD PUBLISHING LTD
Bognor Regis ~ West Sussex ~ England ~ PO21 5EL
www.woodfieldpublishing.co.uk

ISBN 1-84683-098-2

Words and
Wanderings

*An Author's Adventures
at Home and Abroad*

WALLIS PEEL

Woodfield

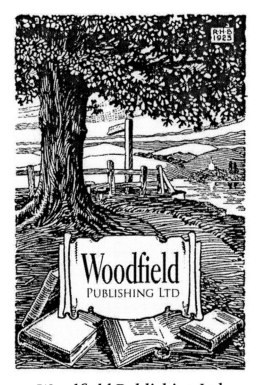

Woodfield Publishing Ltd

Bognor Regis ~ West Sussex ~ PO21 5EL ~ England
tel 01243 821234 ~ **e-mail** enquiries@woodfieldpublishing.co.uk

Interesting and informative books on a variety of subjects

For full details of all our books visit
www.woodfieldpublishing.co.uk

For Roy, my husband of many decades,
who lived two-thirds of this with me

~ CONTENTS ~

Foreword

Hazel Peel is one of those people in life who say what they think and no matter what they get the job done. So reading about the life of someone with that sort of character is always going to be fascinating. I have known Hazel for the almost 20 years and if age has slowed her down during that period (and it will have had to work jolly hard to have slowed Hazel down) I can only imagine what she was like before that. When I first met her she was championing the cause of the public library service, which she values so highly and has used regularly for pleasure and research purposes. She likes nothing more than to set us a challenge of obtaining an old or rare book for her to enjoy reading. In the intervening years and in the wake of the loss of her beloved husband Roy she has thrown herself back in to her own writing once again. Despite recent health problems Hazel has published (and in some cases had republished) a plethora of work from historical novels to local history and horse riding books and children's stories. All of these continue to be very well borrowed from local libraries which has persuaded publishers to produce audio books of many of her titles as well. These very much reflect her own life as a writer of scrupulously researched articles for local newspapers, a lifelong love of horses and someone who enjoys a well-written story.

Neil Weston
Librarian, South Gloucestershire Libraries
June 2010

Hazel Peel is a veteran writer who appeals to readers of all ages. Now aged 80 and with 25 books under her belt she is endearingly modest about her powerful writing skills. But her historical thrillers – they are all more than "novels" – just pull the reader in and are quite unputdownable. Indeed, with Mrs Peel's reliable and thoroughly researched historical facts, her books should be on the school reading list. What better way to get teenagers to enjoy a good read and take in some English history at the same time. While many of her books are set in Roman and Saxon times in her beloved Gloucestershire, Mrs Peel also takes in-depth looks at the years of the Civil War and at the troubled island of Guernsey from 1918 to the German occupation.

Interestingly, one of Hazel Peel's most popular books is the factual *Glorious Gloucestershire*, a useful guide book to this most beautiful and diverse of counties.

Writing as H.M. Peel she also has a stable of children's books, mainly about horses (another of her great loves), which have made her the idol of thousands of youngsters all over the world. All Mrs Peel's books are fluent and exciting – with a pinch of romance here and a dollop of warfare there – an editor's joy and a reader's delight.

Carole J Taylor, Journalist and Editor
June 2010

Hazel Peel's historical fiction is characterised by enthralling plot lines and feisty female characters, but none more feisty than the indomitable Hazel herself. Her autobiography is a cracking good read and an inspiration to women of all ages.

Sara Keane Editor
June 2010

Author's Preface

All my life I have faithfully followed two creeds. "God helps those who help themselves" and (when riding a rough horse at speed and facing an enormous hedge) "Throw your heart over first ... then follow it".

I know what it's like to be poor and hungry but I yearned to travel and see the world. Lack of money never stopped me going anywhere. I had two sound legs and a good right hand for thumbing lifts! If a person yearns to do something shortage of money cannot stop them.

It certainly didn't stop me!

I have always been an avid reader, devouring books. I couldn't live without them. Reading has given me untold pleasure over the years, as has writing.

I wrote this autobiography as a kind of catharsis after losing my beloved husband Roy in 2003 and this book is dedicated to his memory.

Hazel (Wallis) Peel
July 2010

Chapter I

The difference between the Thirties and the 21st century is a similar gulf as that between the Thirties and Victorian times. Social workers deride these so-called 'bad old days' but, despite the hardships for the workers, I know now which I prefer, and for many reasons too. Not least of which, as a pensioner and war widow, is that more respect was given and there was greater safety, especially for us disabled oldies.

I entered this world on the old Whitsuntide Monday at 01.30 hours on 26th May 1930 at Queen Mary's Hospital, West Ham, London. My poor Mother had been days in the most terrible labour and at one stage the doctor took my father to one side and warned him that he might have to choose between his wife and the baby. Without a second's hesitation, my father chose my mother, and good for him too. Obviously, I did eventually make my debut but in so doing my poor Mother was horribly torn, which necessitated major surgery three years later.

When Margaret Thatcher was pushed into premature retirement as Prime Minister she said: "it's a funny old world!" A comment with which I agree. When I look back, I am both amused and amazed at the various ways in which I have earned my living and sometimes they tangle up in confusion. Some were selected with cold deliberation, others were done from the sheer necessity to keep a hungry wolf very much at bay. There were a few which were quite fascinating and others horribly boring but probably the most significant was that into which I drifted quite by chance.

Although I have always been an avid reader, like my parents, it never crossed my mind that I would ever be a published author. Neither did it occur to my parents because publishing books was that which happened to other people, not our humble little family.

My father was Ernest Leslie Charles Wallis, a dyed-in-the-wool Londoner and my mother was Elizabeth Bullen, a true Yorkshire tyke, which meant I had an unusual North/South upbringing that incorporated different points of view, customs and forms of speech. At this time there were most distinctly two separate Englands.

In most families there is a dash of the aristocracy from the wrong side of the blanket. There had long been rumours in the Yorkshire branch that some maternal ancestress hailed from Queen Anne Boleyn, which spelling is only a fancy French version of Bullen. One of my more curious uncles took it upon himself to investigate in his retirement. How he went about this I have no idea, except it took him a long time and eventually he came up with evidence that the rumour was correct. Like a fool, I never thought to delve into this and now it's too late after his death.

On my father's side of the family there is a mysterious blank in the pedigree. One of my male great-greats married a lady who definitely came from the blanket's popular side but nothing else is known.

It is a pity small children cannot remember very early events. I should have a wealth of these because my parents took me to see everything possible especially the Lord Mayor's show and I can remember exactly nothing.

My first true memory is The Bang. To a small child it was a fearful explosion but, oddly enough, neither of my parents remembered it and considered it but a product of a rather fertile, juvenile imagination. Years later, I gave a detailed description of the area of the room from which the Bang emanated and even the location of the door. They were quite staggered and worked out what it was. The culprit was nothing but an internal belch from an antiquated gas geyser in the corner of the room. I was all of two years of age.

My next most vivid memory is of a stagecoach drawn by four wonderful, galloping horses. At this time my parents had moved to Leicester to try to get more reliable work for my father because jobs were very hard to get or hold. My father was a ladies' hairdresser, although he had always wanted to be apprenticed to be an electrician, but his father had vetoed this idea with the explanation that electricity was only a five-day wonder! Gas would always be used for lighting and cooking and ladies would always want their hair attended too. So foolish, so short-sighted, so downright stupid – but in those days, single men did not dare to go against their fathers.

I was the only child of an only child, which was a very peculiar situation in those days. I was adored by my grandparents with whom I went to stay in their minute, rented house in Leytonstone. I remember row upon row of these little box-like homes. The whole area was totally uninteresting to me except for the window of one particular shop. It was the local toy shop and in the centre of the window, holding pride of place, was a perfect model of an American Wells Fargo stagecoach, drawn by four mighty horses. The coach had infinite detail but it was the horse's action that enthralled me.

It was made from lead and the horses were attached to the coach with such skill that even a small child like me could feel power and speed. I adored that coach and horses and my soul craved to own it. Then those marvellous horses would gallop for me. With great eagerness I calculated how long it would take for my Saturday penny to mount up until I had enough to buy this wonderful creation.

It cost the horrendous sum of one shilling and seven pence in pre-decimal coinage. I could just work this out because I was a very advanced reader and had already started to calculate a little.

"Grandpa!" I cried. "That means I have two pennies saved so there will only be another six Saturdays before I can buy it!"

My grandpa looked down at me and sadly shook his head. "You have it all wrong child. A shilling is made up of 12 pennies, which totals to 19 pennies. This means you have to save for another seventeen Saturdays and you won't be here by then."

I was aghast. I distinctly remember how horrified I became. "Oh Grandpa! Can't you buy it for me?" I wailed in frustration.

I can see him now shaking his head firmly. "No child! I don't have money to throw away like that!"

Throw away? How could he say that? Not produce the pennies to buy such an artistic creation? I could hardly believe my ears. He loved me. He had often told me this so surely an important person like a Grandpa had the necessary pennies tucked away somewhere? I knew nothing about loans. What I did know was that I would have beggared my soul to buy that coach and horses. So I learned my first great disappointment in life although it took a long time for this to subside. Even now, umpteen decades later, I can still see that coach and horses and I would love to have it on my desk as I write this.

In those days it was just about unheard of for married woman to work. Only when a family was at absolute rock bottom did the woman go out and try to get a scrubbing job. Mother made all of my clothes and she was a brilliant knitter, which is why I never learned. Her skills were vital because a man's wages had to be eked out to pay the vital living expenses.

At this time my father worked in a West End hairdressing salon and his customers were often stars from the stage.

Sometimes they would give him complimentary tickets and it was with these my parents were able to enjoy a rare treat. Even then, they had to work out the cost of the fares to go "up west", so scarce was money for the working man.

The move to Leicester took place in 1935 and it was a major upheaval. The working classes could not possibly contemplate buying a freehold property so we became the first family to move into a rented house at 1 Berridge Lane. My father had to go straight out to work, leaving my mother coping with collecting water in buckets from a standpipe. I thought this was great fun. Mother did not.

This was the second time my mother had lived in Leicester. She came from a mining family but was very clever with a flair for figures (which she has not passed on to me!). After a traumatic time in her life, about which I learned later, she went out to work as a cashier. Without a doubt Mother was a prime candidate for advanced education but in Yorkshire families in those days, males were more important. They were the ones to go and hew for coal to bring in the 'brass', as money was called in that part of the country. Girls were unimportant, so Mother was denied the higher education to which her brains certainly entitled her. Her teachers wanted her to stay at school, matriculate and go on to university. What a hope. Despite visits from the schools' inspector Grandma Bullen always gave an adamant "no" and that was the end of the matter. Mother was packed off into domestic service with a distant branch of the family in the South, which turned into a miserable existence plus the experience from which she never wholly recovered.

Mother had guts though. She was small with very tiny bones but with the heart of a lion and this she demonstrated throughout her life. I knew her for fifty-three years and her courage gave me my benchmark. After studying in the evenings, she managed to get a job as a clerk with the British United at Leicester. She paddled her own canoe and was very brave indeed in those narrow, hidebound days. She was paid 21 shillings a week. Her rent and board came to 20 shillings and with the shilling left over she wrote home once a week and also paid for night school lessons in shorthand and typing writing. She never had one penny for herself so stoically had to do without everything. Her only great interest was in following the Leicester Tiger rugby players but to watch a game she had to rely upon being given a complimentary ticket or to go as a guest with someone from where she worked.

The British United were so impressed with her they sent her to London to organize their head office, which was a daring move by them. It was while in London she met my father, as they had the mutual interest of tennis and music. How they met, I have no idea – and proper thing too. My father played football but used to get many injuries and in those harsh employment days he dared not take time off from work so he had to give up his sport.

Our new home in Leicester was fringed with lovely countryside which appealed to me greatly. Mother used to take me for long walks by the banks of the River Soar, which carried many leeches in its water. I was both repelled and fascinated by them, goodness only knows why. Children can get weird and wonderful fancies.

It was on these walks I started to learn about our countryside, the trees, plants, flowers and wildlife. My mother had a fund of natural knowledge, which she passed down to me, though I was never very good at identifying trees like her. Father was a real street-bred Londoner. Take him away from basic grass and he was quite lost. He could recognise a dandelion but that was his lot.

It was while we lived here that our little family expanded. One-day, while out walking, my mother saw a woman hauling along on a piece of string a miserable, half-starved silver grey Alsatian bitch. She was thin to the point of being gaunt and the picture of canine misery. My mother stopped to talk.

"This dog is a nuisance. We can't afford to feed her."

Even to my young eyes that was obvious and my mother thought the same. I flashed her a hopeful look.

"I'll have her!" my mother said.

The woman was momentarily stunned. "You will? Here! She's yours!" and the tacky string was thrust into Mother's hand. So began my love affair with all animals. She became my best pal for many happy years and I have never had regard for any other dog as I had for Bo, as we christened her.

We all loved her, especially my father, who was a real animal person. Before I came upon the scene, they owned a rough, wire-haired terrier, which suddenly turned savage for no reason whatsoever. One day my father bent to pat the dog, which leapt at his face and savaged him. The terrier, of course, had to be put down. After her came Rita, also an Alsatian, but she had something wrong with her internally so she too had to be put to sleep. The arrival of Bo delighted my father although it meant the precious pennies were forced to stretch even farther.

Bo was so hungry when we arrived back home she hastily gobbled some potato peelings. My mother was livid and so was father when he heard. He was better with animals than people and, to a certain extent, so am I. Dogs talked to father and it was only many decades later he became friendly with the cat, our first cat, a seal point Siamese who had an incredible character and could be highly entertaining.

I was never lonely even as an only child. Apart from the fact I had my pal Bo I had wonderful books, which were a magical world to me. I was a very advanced reader for my age, possibly because my nose was always stuck in a book. My parents were huge readers and I followed their example with enormous delight and pleasure. We all belonged to a lending library and in those days there were many, not just the normal council libraries.

There were always masses of books at home and every one was treasured. Nothing was ever withheld from me as a child. My parents went to great pains to explain words which were beyond my limited years and they taught me how to use a dictionary. No matter how tough the times were, and they could be exceedingly bad in the Thirties, a few pennies were always carefully saved to buy a second-hand book. I was taught to treat them with great respect. To dog-ear a page was just about a criminal offence. Today when I pick up a library book and find pages dog-eared I have a rush of blood to the head with anger. A bookmark is so simple to make or even a slip torn off the newspaper.

Life was very harsh in the mid-thirties. Jobs were most precarious to hold and the men who had them treated them like gold because each position had three men waiting to fill it. There were no State benefits then and the Old Age pension was just ten shillings a week. It was a small sum handed out very grudgingly and it was Means Tested very harshly. Poverty was not a crime because there were simply too many people who knew what that word meant. Yet real crime was hardly known. Doors were left unlocked and burglaries were incredibly rare.

It was then my parents took the most enormous gamble for people of their class. They searched their hearts, examined their tiny bit of money, decided to borrow and buy a little business and be independent. They borrowed from family, never moneylenders with their exorbitant rates of interest. All his life Grandpa Wallis had worked as a labourer for the water authority, which was a guaranteed position for life. Not for him the trauma of the dole queue, so he had laboriously saved a little money.

My parents bought a dear little grocery shop at 35 West Avenue, Clarendon Park, Leicester. The idea was that Mother would work the shop while father would open a hairdressing salon in their large downstairs room. It was a horrible gamble but they were determined to try to haul themselves onto the next rung of the ladder. In those days, class was the be all and end all of society with rigid demarcation lines and the worst offender was the working class.

The shop did not have a garden but a large yard at the rear with a stable. It was here that Bo and I played happily together. At the bottom of Cecelia Road ran the trams into the city, from the terminus not far away. It was a swift and cheap way to get into the city for the market, though in good weather, like many others, we walked to save money.

Nearby was the huge Victoria Park, which contained acres of lovely grassland dominated by the World War I War Memorial, built in the style of the Arc de Triumph in Paris. This was the people's playground because holidays as such did not exist – except for the rich.

On summer Sundays we would walk to the park and spend nearly a whole day there with our sandwiches, even though it was less than half a mile from our home. It was so large it was simple to get away from people and forget the rows of streets.

In the winter we made our own entertainment when not reading. We had our radio and my parents listened to certain programs, especially the news and those involving music. We played card games, my favourite of which was rummy and for my parents, when they could get another pair, whist. They tried to teach me the latter but whist and bridge have always been mysteries to me. Many years later on I learned chess and became reasonably good at it. Draughts was another popular game for us. Father fixed a dartboard to a door but my early efforts did not do the paintwork much good, so he had to put it in a frame.

We had a piano because music was important to my parents and it had been a wedding present from paternal grandparents. My mother was a very good player while father's instrument was the euphonium. In their early married days in London father had his own five-piece band. It was only an amateur group but they gave great pleasure and produced valuable money. Father was skilled in that he could take a piece of sheet music and write it out for a wind instrument then transpose it for Mother's piano. Music was a great joy for them and they had high hopes for me. Alas it was not to be!

While at the shop they scraped up the money for me to have piano lessons at the stupendous cost of two shillings and sixpence an hour. They could only afford one lesson a week but I was expected to practice for at least one hour a day. I hated it. I did learn to murder some pieces of music on that long-suffering piano then my parents saw the light and realised their folly. Music lessons were stopped to my great delight. Since then I have only really enjoyed music when it has been associated with something pleasurable in the past.

I was an active little girl. My mother learned to swim at an early age and at 11 years she swam a recorded mile, which was a tremendous feat in 1915. Father had been pretty good on the football field and tennis was their summer sport when they were young. Father could not swim and did not want to know. Mother tried to teach him but he simply turned blue in the sea and that was that.

My parents were fairly well matched although poles apart in temperament as well as the North/South divide. Was it a good marriage? I think so, though it is hard to say when viewed from a great distance. I know my father never had any interest in other females unless they had four legs and could bark. Probably they simply rubbed along because divorce was OUT for the working class, who had no money for such in the first place. Each would savagely defend the other from derogatory remarks so I suppose it was quite a good match.

I had a lot of fun playing in the streets, of which there were rows upon boring rows. Most of them had front doors which opened directly onto the pavement. They usually had a handkerchief of a back garden where a few vegetables and flowers would struggle to exist.

I preferred to play with the boys. Oddly enough, there were not many girls in the immediate streets around West Avenue and of these only a few could reach my tomboy antics. I considered them all cissies who cried for their mothers at the drop of a hat. Boys were more adventurous, more fun to be with and better company in my eyes.

Children's street games were very serious and played only at specific times of year. An adult did not need a calendar; all he had to do was remember back to his own childhood and see which games were being played. It was unheard of for certain games to be played in the incorrect season and children, being tribal by instinct, adhered religiously to this unwritten constitution.

One of the most popular games was that with cigarette cards. In those days cigarette manufacturers placed a picture card in every cigarette packet. These could be collected in sets and today are worth a small fortune to collectors. All the children saved 'fag cards', as they were known in street language and they became a children's currency with trading rules which rivalled anything on the Stock Exchange. Every child regularly scoured the gutters for empty packets in the hope an adult would have left the card inside. No man could take his last cigarette in the streets without a child hovering to beg the card. Shops which specialized in selling cigarettes and tobacco always had a collection of children loitering hopefully nearby.

The game of fag cards was played by balancing one card on its edge against a brick wall. From an agreed distance players flicked their own cards at the one which was leaning. The object was to knock it flat. When this had been achieved, the player in question could collect ALL the cards lying around. Competition and rivalry were fierce. Certain cards were carefully glued back-to-back to make a 'king' card. When this extra thick card was flicked it could produce a devastating effect on the leaning card if the throw had been accurate. Of course, if the aim was poor it meant a precious 'king' card now lay on the pavement. When this happened the competition really hotted up. There was tremendous street cred in gaining another's 'king' card, to say nothing of the value.

Marbles was another game played on the same principle of knocking another's marble at an agreed distance or angle. When achieved, all the other marbles which lay around became trophies. Sometimes the marbles were called 'alleys' although this name usually referred to extra-large, powerful marbles often of many colours and great beauty. It was heartbreaking for a child to lose a large alley in marble combat. Large alleys were worth a small fortune on the youthful financial market and the loss of one could push a child almost to bankruptcy. A prudent child only used a large alley when certain of victory.

In the Autumn we played conkers. Today the asinine politically correct brigade want to ban this game in case children are hurt. I have never heard such stupid piffle in all my life! All through my childhood I played conkers in the autumn, along with most other children. I never heard of anyone receiving even a minor bruise.

The locations of horse chestnut trees, far and wide, were known to us although in our heavily built-up area it could mean a lot of walking to reach one. No park or garden was safe from trespass if it happened to have a horse chestnut tree. Sticks, stones and other missiles were hurled into the foliage to bring down specific conkers because those on the ground were often considered substandard.

A hole was carefully drilled through the conker's centre, a string threaded through and knotted at the conker's end. The idea was to smash your conker at that of your opponent to break it. Many a conker was made hard by the simple expedient of a short time in a hot oven! A clever youthful financier might exchange a winning conker for a 'king' fag card with a view to long-term plans for when next playing fag cards.

'Whip and top' was another very important seasonal game which required considerable skill to make the wooden top travel along the pavement, constantly spinning, without falling on its side. Both sexes played whip and top though hoopla was a pure girl's game. A thin hoop, as large as a bicycle wheel, was whipped along with taps from a light cane. This also was a highly skilful and delicate game which was probably why the boys avoided it.

Another favourite girl's game was hopscotch. For this the flagstones on the pavement had to be used and marked out in a set pattern with chalk – which did not greatly please the adults. Some of the housewives kept their pavements scrubbed, they were so house-proud.

The object of this game was to move from one square to the other on one leg only in a preordained pattern. At the end the girl had to turn around, still only on one leg, and hop back, chanting a mantra. The boys scorned such a game but we girls suspected it was because they lacked the skill to win at it and dared not lose face before us!

Skipping was another cherished girl's game and here tremendous skill and agility were needed. The skips could be one or two legged, blindfolded, bent over or in other crazy positions. Sometimes the skip was performed with one twirl of the rope but in the more complicated rites, the girl's jump had to be high enough to account for two twirls of the rope. Any boxer in training could have taken lessons from some of these girls. Skipping was always performed to ritual songs, the words of which I have sadly forgotten. A girl never skipped in silence. This was simply not done.

An indoors girl's game was 'snobs', although in other parts of the country it might be called 'gobs'. This game could be played solo like the card game of patience or with a group. The object was to cast the snobs into the air and catch them with one snob tucked into the palm of the hand. Those that landed MUST be caught on the knuckles. There were variations of this game, which increased in complexity. Two snobs would be caught on the knuckles and even three and sometimes the four. Only infants were allowed to catch the snobs in the palm of their hand. Many, many decades later, I still have a set of rather battered snobs and can play – a little.

Chapter II

As an only child I was lucky with my toys because my father was very clever with his hands. What my parents could not afford to buy he simply made. There was a special purse kept for toys for me and into this would go a spare penny now and again. These toys I remember with great affection. There was a wonderful, bright red rocking horse, a red pedal car, a red scooter and even if they did come to me a bit battered after another child's use, that mattered not to me. Somehow my parents managed to scrape up the money to buy me a two wheeled fairy cycle but for some strange reason I hated it. I would not even go near it so my parents managed to resell it without too great a loss. A few years later they acquired an adult's sit-up-and-beg cycle and I jumped on it straight away and rode it as if I had been doing it for years. Kids can be very queer creatures.

Toys were well made then, from wood or metal. They were gaily painted, solid and quite indestructible. They were objects which endured and in large families were carefully handed down again and again. Mine did eventually go to distant cousins. When very young I had a huge teddy bear, just about as big as myself and two enormous china pot dolls. They left me cold and I ignored them, much to my parents' chagrin. I preferred boys' toys. I could do so much more with them and my imagination knew no bounds. I had wonderful lead soldiers and animals whose colours, detail and sheer solidity put today's plastic rubbish to shame.

One Christmas Father produced a fort. Another year it was a doll's house but this was never put to the use for which it had been intended. By the time I had finished it resembled the Alamo and so did the battles which took place there.

Then there was the train set. My father arranged this and it took up a lot of saving. It was clockwork because an electric model was too costly. Precious pennies were put aside every week so that another piece of equipment could be purchased. There were bridges, signals, level crossings, little lead porters carrying luggage as well as passengers awaiting the train. There were three locomotives of Hornby 'O' gauge which today, as collector's items, would be worth a fortune. I adored this and so did my father! The only snag was it had to be put down then lifted and packed away after each day's play. There simply was not the room to leave a layout down.

Near the shop, a few streets away in another direction, were freehold properties whose children went to private schools. These families departed once a year on holiday. They were as far apart from us as the North Pole. I did get to know one boy slightly and he had an electric train set which was left down permanently. It was this above all else which showed the difference in our financial status. I was not jealous though; this has, luckily, never been one of my failings. I knew in comparison I was incredibly well off to my friends who roamed the streets with me. Socialising and making a close friendship with someone from another class was very much frowned upon by all sides.

The Wallis grandparents always brought me a toy when they visited – although never that wonderful coach and horses. Even today as an old person I can look back and see every detail and wonder who did eventually own it. They would not have treasured it as much as I would have done then and now.

Grandma Wallis had really missed out in life because of the stupidity of her father, Daniel Rackstraw. He had been a Guardsman and then became a city of London policeman. These men had to be a very tall and because of his job,

Grandma and her sisters, were all born within the city of London just about next door to Bow Bells. They were real London cockneys. Because of this particular location these four girls became entitled to a superior education and the freedom of the city of London. Their idiotic father refused both saying "they are only girls!" Who knows what might not have happened and where those four Rackstraw girls might have ended up. Probably quite high indeed.

Upon grave reflection it seems all the males in the Wallis family were neither bold nor outgoing. Mother and the Bullen tribe were the exact opposite. Mother would weigh up a situation, calculate the risk then act. Prior to my arrival Mother had worked it out that with care and prudence, they could – just – manage to scrape up enough money to put a deposit on a freehold house. My father was totally horrified. Why *buy* a house when one could rent one? He had been brainwashed by his timid father. The working classes had always paid rent and he would not budge from this. It was a ghastly error but it took years for him to realize this. Whenever there were rows between my parents it was always over my mother's boldness and my father's timidity. They were temperamental opposites doomed forever to clash.

Divorce was quite out of the question. A couple married, made their bed and had to get on with it. In the 21st century divorce appears to be an expected rite with single parents proliferating. Which is better, a stormy marriage with the couple jointly rearing the children or single parents battling alone? I do not know.

Father's manual dexterity was not confined to toy making. He had large hands with spatulate, clumsy looking fingers but what clever hands they were. Although trained as a hairdresser he did still yearn to be an electrician. In many houses in which we lived, especially before World War II, the only light came from dismal gas mantles. This never bothered father. He simply disconnected the gas and wired up the house himself. What I now know was remarkable was that he had never had an official lesson in his life. He just knew how to handle electricity. The end result was always the same. The local electricity authority would find out, throw a fit and descend to condemn his efforts. They always ended up not being able to fault a thing and offering father a job with them. It was all too late though. The drums of war had started to sound and Father had been brainwashed by his father in that the only 'proper' way to make a living was as a ladies' hairdresser.

The main route of this Wallis hesitancy was a genuine fear of that ugly word 'debt'. No decent person, no matter how poor, would go into debt if they could help it. Nothing was bought until it could be paid for. No tally or pawn shops for either side of the family. A debt was nothing but an instrument of the devil!

During this period I saw the maternal side of the family only infrequently. Sometimes they would come and visit although Mother's younger brother Arthur never left us long and neither did Uncle Bob. 'Visiting' was important. It was considered a highly necessary ritual with certain understood and enforced codes of conduct. One always visited at least once a year, come hell or high water and one simply never went empty-handed. It did not matter the value of the gift as long as there was something, nearly always in the form of food or drink. A jar of home-made jam would suffice or six new-laid eggs. It was the ritual which counted.

At this young age I did not take much notice of visitors. Uncle Arthur did, for a time, work at the dreaded workhouse, a ghastly place where people were stripped of their dignity and privacy, a place where, in reality, it was better to be dead. He had always been interested in medical matters but, like the rest of the Bullen males, he was sent to work down the coal mine at Wath Main. He was strong minded enough to break from this mould and eventually joined the Royal Army Medical Corps as a regular soldier.

The Bullen grandparents always bothered me. I held them in considerable awe and even quite a lot of fear. They were different to the other adults I knew at Leicester and children don't like this. They spoke in another way, with a heavy South Yorkshire accent and used words which were strange to me though Mother understood them easily enough. It was my first experience of coping with a dialect. Their views were certainly not mine and at this stage of life I was distinctly uneasy with them. It was not until I became older that my visits became more frequent and I began to slip into their way of life in all respects.

Like many children I snooped because I was nosy. One-day, just before the war, I poked around in a drawer where I had no business to be. At the bottom I found a long, brown envelope and inside was a mysterious document. Naturally I took it out and because I was such an advanced reader the legal language did not really throw me too much, though some of the will's words made me stumble. What did puzzle me was the fact that the document stated quite clearly that Uncle Bob was adopted.

I had enough sense not to blurt out my questions to my parents when they came home, although I buzzed with curiosity. From where did Uncle Bob come then and why? It was to be quite a few years before I learned the truth. Meanwhile I pushed it all to the back of my mind because there was so much to do in life.

At the same time I became aware that my parents would often be talking animatedly but cease on my appearance. I was far too young and ignorant to even begin to understand matters political and the threat of an impending war with Germany.

Bo was my best friend and shadow and she too had a pal who would come and call. Calling followed one pattern only.

The child simply stood outside the house and called loudly for their friend. No one knocked. That was for grown-ups only. Bo's friend was a black and tan Alsatian owned by a family friend. He would come around and bark outside the door until it was opened and he could enter to frolic with Bo. We all had a great amusement from this.

In those distant days violence was just about unheard of. Old people were certainly not mugged for their purses let alone for kicks. Murders were exceedingly rare and shocking when they did happen. One never heard of babies being battered or abused though of course probably some were. The word paedophile had not yet been invented. People were poor but more civilized because they had both pride and dignity. Children could walk to school and play in the streets without fear of molestation. A policeman was someone to be respected and if he clipped one's ear for an offence the culprit knew father would add another couple for good measure. Property was respected especially trees, flower gardens and the parks as these were places to be enjoyed by all. Not ruined by a selfish, spiteful handful of hoodlums. Graffiti was quite unheard of. Today's stupid, do-gooders should read back about those days and grow up themselves. Perhaps their ridiculous, politically correct ideals will change when they become old and are mugged in turn.

Women though were just about second-class citizens with many openings still denied to them, a ridiculous hangover from the Victorians which only another war would remove completely. The women who did go out to work were usually single and even then could become the subject of much gossip. Even if a woman did break in to the man's world of business she most certainly did not receive his salary even when doing the same job, injustice just waiting to be swept away, all of which was long overdue for change, modernization and equality.

It was in the late 30s that Grandpa Wallis died. He had suffered from Parkinson's disease for many years but the actual cause of death was pneumonia. Father went alone to the all-male funeral. Grandma had been left a few hundred pounds from insurances which, by our classes' standard, made her almost affluent. Sad to say though, without Grandpa's restraining influence she could not handle this money and it simply vanished somewhere. So she came to live with us, which was not exactly a howling success.

Two women of different generations can rarely make it work in the kitchen and when they also descend from different cultures the mix can be explosive. The atmosphere at home was not really thrilling so I simply retreated even more into my beloved books. I was safe with them and above family rows.

I neither liked nor disliked school. It was simply a place where all children had to go, rather like fathers had to go to work – if they were lucky enough to have a job. School then was totally different to that of the 21st century. Discipline was rigidly enforced, with a cane if necessary, as were morals and manners.

Children in class, unless actively reading or writing, had to sit up straight with arms folded. Talking was strictly forbidden and children did not dare to speak unless spoken to first. Boys were caned on a regular basis. Girls were considered too weak for this so they were humiliated in public before the whole school. I have no idea whether this was good or bad but we grew up with a code of conduct even though we were not saints by any standards.

The three Rs – reading, writing and arithmetic – were dinned into us. Multiplication tables had to be learned by rote, which was nothing but brainwashing, yet I can still remember most of them, so how harmful was this? We received a very good grounding in history, geography and religion. We were also taught 'joined up' writing and this had to be neat and minus blots. I had a lovely hand which I promptly lost when I went to the next school where speed was of the essence and not calligraphy.

We had to march to classes, not walk, and quietly too. Playtime was ten minutes morning and afternoon when all hell then broke loose in the playground. Anything was allowed except fighting and one unfortunate teacher always had to be present.

At this time most children received some kind of religious education outside school known as Sunday school. Attendance was just about obligatory and for this we received a stamp. This was stuck on a card and, when full, the child became entitled to go on the church outing. Leicester is in the centre of the country so the town selected was always Skegness.

Holidays were unheard of for the working-class in the Thirties because lack of money and the ability of the male breadwinner to take time off work. Some other large factories would shut down for a week and if people had paid into a club, they might be lucky enough to have a cheap seaside holiday somewhere. This was especially true of northern parts of the country. The day's outing from Sunday school was spoken of with awe for weeks in advance and made one of the great red-letter days of the year.

Grandma Wallis had always been a member of the Salvation Army and for one short period of my childhood she persuaded me to become a Sunbeam. Even now this memory raises a chuckle because I was the most un-sunbeam-like child one could hope to find.

Nevertheless, I liked going to these small social events because Grandma Wallis was brilliant at recitation. She was quite deaf yet had a first-class memory and an excellent vocal tone. This was a very popular form of simple entertainment and she was in great demand.

I gradually dropped the Salvation Army, although I have always held these officers and men with the greatest respect and I never fail to buy their *War Cry* when I see one for sale. When one considers their history and how and why they came into being, their battle call of 'Blood and Fire' is most appropriate. Running a religious order on military grounds was pure genius. Their music is outstanding – and this statement is made by someone who is not musical.

I enjoyed going into Mother's part of the shop, especially when a representative or 'traveller' appeared. These men, and they were always men too, were no fools. They would spread out their sweet wares on the highly polished counter and take note of my likes and dislikes. I was usually allowed free rein with the samples so the adults were able to work out juvenile requirements.

Mother always made her own ice cream and very good it was. When we went to the Victoria Park for a day out in the summer, part of the treat was always to buy an ice cream from the Walls' man. He rode a heavy cycle emblazoned with the legend "STOP ME AND BUY ONE." The ice cream was carried in a huge container on the front of the cycle and kept cold with dry ice. Father used to buy four because, naturally, Bo had her ice cream as well. I have never met a dog yet who doesn't adore ice cream and quite a few of our cats, later on in my life, also enjoyed a couple of spoonfuls.

Mother packed her ice cream drum with dry ice, inside of which also went mysterious ingredients. Then she would churn and churn watched by an audience of two. Me and Bo. We were always allowed to have the scrapings and I swear Mother's ice cream was every bit as good as that from Walls.

Motor cars were so rare they invited staring when they did appear. Trams and buses made a good public transport and most families had a beat up cycle. Goods were transported by horse and cart or a horse-drawn van. Enterprising children followed these with a bucket and shovel to collect the horse manure to sell for pennies. Potential capitalists who knew a good thing when they saw one.

Horses fascinated me as they had done since that day with the toy coach and horses in Leytonstone. I vividly remember one red letter day. Out of the blue a lady appeared in our streets actually riding a horse. It was probably only a small pony but it appeared gigantic to me. This was an event which quite equalled man's landing on the moon. What on earth she was doing riding in an area of such crowded, humble streets I have never understood and still don't.

All of us children ran up to stare with goggle-eyed amazement at this incredible apparition. I was bold like my mother and I stepped forward, my eyes mesmerised, then looked up at the Lady rider.

"Can I have a ride please?" I asked politely and hopefully.

The lady looked down at me with lofty snootiness and did not even bother to reply. She probably saw a filthy, scruffy little girl with a gang of boys and that was all. She lacked the perception to see the love and longing in my eyes. She was too obtuse to understand what it would have meant to let me climb into the saddle and just be led along the street. Heaven would have been mine for this simple gesture which would have cost her nothing but a few seconds of her time.

She turned her mount and walked away. If the boys had not been present I would have burst into tears but crying before the boys was simply NOT done. They regarded me as a bit of a tough kid even though I was a mere girl and they were wary of me. Probably with good reason.

In those days boys did not hit girls because their code of conduct banned this, a code perfectly sensible and understood to all children but quite incomprehensible to adults. If a boy thought a girl meant a row with him he simply stalked away. William, of the great William books, had this particular problem with Violet Elizabeth Bott!

I was that rare individual – a member of a boys' gang and as such I must never show tears. Children's gangs in those days were very innocent gatherings. Today in the 21st century they are horrendous affairs, full of violence and wickedness in which even 13 and 14 year olds carry knives and will not hesitate to use them. They will also use anything else capable of trying to kill like claw hammers, as has come out in the courts. How much simpler were our little gangs of the Thirties.

I knew I was greatly privileged to belong to a boys' gang and there was no ardent trade unionist more dedicated than me. For it meant so much more fun. Their games were wilder and more exciting. They ventured farther afield and I was considered a good member of the gang. I did not mind bloodied knees, cut hands and even the odd accidental black eye (tumbles and falls produced the most weird injuries) for these were gang wounds and worn with pride like medals. They always produced trouble at home but such was a mere bagatelle when compared to the honour of being a member of a boys' gang.

Some of us were the proud owners of ball bearing roller skates and we would rush to the park to race around the War Memorial on the flat paving stones, shrieking with glee to the fury of the park warden. We shared our skates with the poorer boys, in the spirit of gang democracy or a kind of Freemasonry.

'The pictures' were the working class's escapism and everyone went at least once a week, as the program was always changed mid-week. There would be a documentary, a Movietone newsreel, and then the main feature film. The picture house was an important social structure, even if some of the adult goings-on in the back row were questionable.

Because of the religious influences at home, ours was just about a teetotal house. I cannot remember either of my parents ever setting foot in a pub. I only have a vague memory of a bottle of cheap wine on the table on Christmas Day. Because of this I did not set foot in a pub until I was twenty one years old, which must be some kind of record.

The main reason, apart from the lack of money, was the fear of what drink could do. It could lead a person into the dreaded debt and therefore all drink had to be – very bad. Grandma Bullen in Yorkshire was a Methodist and a very strict teetotaller but the family males were rebels and would have none of this. It was not until I became adult that I fully understood the genuine family fear.

Going to the pictures was fantasy and escapism, for most people did not have terribly happy lives. The glamour on the silver screen became their dream. A good back seat cost ninepence and seats at the front ranged from fourpence to sixpence – and this was at a time when £2.10.0 was considered a stupendous wage for a working man. On Saturday mornings the picture houses were all given over to children, which must have been unmitigated hell for the staff.

My pocket money had risen to the dizzy height of six pennies, handed to me every Saturday but for which I had to do jobs. It was dinned into me that nothing came from nothing; all had to be earned. My jobs entailed cleaning all the downstairs windows as well as the cutlery. Even the boys did not escape work for there Saturday spending money. They would have to bring in the coal, clean shoes or run errands. Those were the days of domestic demarcation to rival anything later dreamed up by trade unions. No man in his right mind would pick up a duster and no woman with a brain in her head would carry coal or clean shoes.

Even when I had my six pennies I could not do as I liked with them which I considered grossly unfair but I was helpless to remedy the situation. Two pennies had to be handed back 'to be saved'. I had a post office bank book and when six pennies had accumulated, every three Saturdays, it had to be paid into my account. I was not at all enthusiastic about this but had no option on the matter. It was, of course, an excellent way to teach thrift to a child and I have always managed to save something, no matter how small from my wage.

What I did with the remaining four pennies was my affair. Two pennies went on sweets and here and I had the marvellous advantage of the shop. I had to buy my sweets like any other child although I was allowed to have broken or damaged ones at half price. I knew what was in every jar and box because I had peeped. The boy members of the gang knew I was allowed to purchase such goods cheap which made me a MOST valuable gang member. In my naivety it never entered my head that this was obviously the real reason I had been allowed to join the gang in the first place. Naturally, I always looked after my comrades when it came to spending those wonderful Saturday pennies.

The gang always had an undisputed leader who was the best fighter though not necessarily the biggest boy. He had to prove his worth to lead the gang with fists. Boot fighting and kicking was totally banned as unsporting and outside the boys' code of conduct. Every gang leader had a valued and treasured Lieutenant, often the next best fighter, in the juvenile pecking order. I was only a girl but I could use my fists as well. It was out of the question for me to lead a boys' gang so I became a surrogate lieutenant. I was deferred to as well because I had it in me to bloody a boy's nose if the need arose. With the hindsight of maturity the cunning of the young male mind amuses me. It was all those cheap sweets without a shadow of a doubt.

When all the Saturday jobs were finished and our money received we were free to do what we liked in the morning. It was always the same – the children's picture house. Great favourites were Flash Gordon, Hopalong Cassidy, with his lovely horse, and Johnny Weissmuller as Tarzan of the Apes.

Children did not just watch the films, they lived each and every frame. We cheered the hero and booed the villain. We became hysterical with delight when peril crept up behind the hero's back and we nearly died a thousand deaths when each serial ended with a cliff-hanger. How could we possibly live another seven days before learning what happened? The noise from the cinema, jam-packed with exciting children, must have been out of this world. What it did to the attendants' nerves I now shudder to think. Do today's children get quite as much fun and excitement with their electronic games and computers? I bet not.

For a time there were singing cowboys and how unpopular these were. Gene Autry and Roy Rogers might have made themselves quite a bit of money but it never came from juvenile admirers. I only liked to watch Roy Rogers because he always rode stunning palomino horses just as Buck Jones always rode a grey, incorrectly labelled white.

Films were rigidly certified and it was customary for children to try to sneak into adults' films. "Take me in please Mister?" would be the question, and most adults would oblige. But this could be a risky business for girls, as I found out. One day a man took me in but insisted I sat next to him. After a while he went about the old flashing trick. I lacked the knowledge and confidence to grab hold of it and yank it off! I was sick, frightened and just did not know what to do – what little girl does? I opened my mouth ready to scream and the man bolted from the cinema. I did not dare tell my parents, as I would have been banned from setting foot in such a place again.

There was a second time when getting into the cinema this way backfired on me. The film was *Beau Geste* and the opening frames showed corpses around the fort's wall. Even when so young I had a vivid imagination. Fortunately, that day I sat by myself, no gang member was present because I would have ended up drummed right out of the gang for all time. For a few seconds I sat in that totally packed cinema frozen with fear, gazing at those bodies. Then I leapt from my seat, belted back up the aisle, screaming my head off at the highest decibel level my lungs would allow. For a while there was general pandemonium and a good half of the adult audience must have had a heart attack. Nothing would get me back inside that cinema ever again. Many years later, as an adult, I saw the film once more and chuckled over those opening shots that had so terrified me.

A children's great favourite of the time was *Tarzan of the Apes* and there have been many actors taking this role since then but I don't think any of them ever matched the performances of Johnny Weismuller. He played the part to perfection and those films had no equal for many years until *Greystoke* was made. When we came out of the pictures, the streets became our jungle, reverberating with ghastly imitations of Tarzan's calls.

Chapter III

Christmas was the time for great fun, especially in the build up to the actual day. I would go to bed on Christmas Eve almost sick with nerves and anticipation, quite convinced I would never sleep. I would expectantly hang an empty pillowcase at the foot of my bed. It never entered my head that I was a lucky little girl. Some of the gang members did not even bother to hang up a stocking because they knew they would receive exactly nothing. Perhaps a few would have a penny wrapped up in silver paper with an orange or an apple but that would be their lot.

I never did see my parents sneak into my room. I would awaken at some ungodly hour on Christmas morning and there would be a bulging pillowcase. I would scramble from my bed, drag this over and plunge wildly inside. What treasures I would find! Most would only have cost a few pennies because father would have worked on them with those clever hands of his. A few might have been bought over the year and hidden on the top of a wardrobe. The books would be second-hand ones which had been cleaned up but each of which was cherished.

As I was given so was I taught to give, even though my gifts were very humble. In the run-up to Christmas I was even excused putting those two pennies away as savings. I might have found a pretty comb somewhere or a cheap little trinket ornament. It did not matter as long as I too gave.

Most of my books were about animals and the countryside and they always included at least one Romany book. These were written by George Bramwell Evans, a full-blooded Romany. He was a genius at creating natural history for children in his fiction books. I was not alone in adoring Romany and eventually had the full collection of his books, which were handed on, regretfully, to cousins when I was adult and moving around. There was Romany himself, his dog Raq and the boy Tim. When Romany died suddenly from a heart attack, the children of Britain were devastated. Schools had to close as pupils were distraught. No man can have a finer epitaph, surely? Today we have brilliant naturalists like Sir David Attenborough and Professor David Bellamy who are admired and respected, but do today's young have the love for them that we had for Romany?

Mother was a superb cook. Her meals were a sheer delight even when she had to use the cheapest of ingredients. Food was different then, it tasted better. None of today's chemicals. People were ignorant about vitamins and fibre while the range of products available was miniscule compared to that of a modern supermarket.

Cooking was done differently as well. Nothing was ever grilled. I can only remember my mother using the grill to warm the plates. Thick animal fat like dripping was used for frying and roasting and we only had fruit when it came into season, the same with greens. Yet somehow we thrived. Salads were unheard of apart from a limp lettuce and motheaten tomatoes. They were scorned as pure rabbit food.

We had neither fridges nor freezers, nor modern gadgets so housework was sheer hard labour. Food had to be purchased on a daily basis because even a cold slate slab did not keep food for many hours. Milk was delivered daily and would be stored under a red, unglazed pot which kept it cool enough to last a whole day. It wasn't pasteurized either. It came in pint bottles with a cardboard top which was always removed carefully by little girls. These tops, when cleaned up, were perfect for making pom-poms.

Thousands of little shops proliferated, each of which competed fiercely for the housewives' custom. A portion of each day was set aside by the housewife for 'the shopping'. One received both manners and service and nothing was ever too much trouble for the shop assistants. The reason was simple; their jobs were always at stake with a queue for any vacancies.

Butter came in enormous half-hundredweight blocks and the butter required would-be chopped from this with a knife, shaped with wooden spatulas then weighed. The shop assistants were so skilled and fast they could chop off one pound in weight at one go. It would be put into greaseproof paper then, with a couple of hand twirls, fastened into a fancy packet. Tea was also weighed on demand from large wooden chests and this applied to other dry goods like flour, sugar and dried fruits. No one drank coffee, it was virtually unheard of. I was in my late teens before I had my first cup of coffee and was promptly hooked.

We did not have shop biscuits at home because they were too expensive so Mother might make a few now and again. Her cakes were marvellous. Sunday dinner was quite a ritual. There would always be a roast joint, as large as could be afforded which ranged from beef, lamb or pork although it was usually beef because this was the cheapest meat. There was always Yorkshire pudding, roast potatoes and one green vegetable. We never had a starter, which was considered unnecessary, but we did always have a magnificent, filling and stodgy pudding, accompanied with custard.

These were gorgeous. Mother's suet puddings were a dream of delight. Father had a passion for fruit pies but had a sweet tooth so they had to be drowned in sugar. We ate everything they now tell us not to eat, yet we survived. We never had cream; that was only for the rich. Afterwards there was always tea to drink, again with a lot of sugar.

The main meal was at midday, lunch did not exist for the working class. The last meal of the day was tea, which would always be substantial, with plenty of bread and butter and whatever was going. There was always a home-made cake or buns with which to finish. We never ate supper in our family; that would have been considered gluttony and another sin from the devil.

The kettle was kept permanently on the hob of the coal fire, ready to make constant cups of tea, which were drunk throughout the day. Our heating was the open coal fire and they all had a little side trivet on which to rest the precious kettle. We did not have milk drinks at night although some families did. On rare occasions there might be a mug of cocoa but made from water with just a tiny splash of milk.

Breakfast was a proper meal. Cereal, fried egg and bacon with toast and home-made jam or marmalade. My father asserted that the day could not start properly without a cooked breakfast. We ate very well. Many families did not. Children in particular were undernourished and rickets was a common condition to see as well as scurvy, lice and fleas.

Some of the most fascinating shops were the co-operatives known as the Co-ops. The staff were always men who wore long, spotlessly-clean white smocks. A boy would start as the general dogsbody but if he had what it took he could work himself up into the position of general manager, which was a plum job. The Co-ops could pick and choose because their standards were very high.

Money never crossed a palm at a co-op because they all had the same system. Wires were strung all over the ceilings which came down to each assistant. From just above each man's head there was a long handle and a container with a screw base. The money was placed in this, the handle pulled sharply and the container would skid over the wire to a central cash desk. Both change and receipt would return the same way.

Each customer had a dividend number and always gave this when paying. The receipt would confirm this number. Twice a year there would be a payout of dividends, which amounted to a few pence in the pound. The amount varied in different parts of the country. Taken on a six-monthly basis this was a welcome bonus for the domestic economy. Dividend payout day was always a red-letter day.

Life at home was very hard for the housewives. No electrical goods and coal fires make an awful lot of mess. The new-fangled vacuum cleaner was only for the upper-class. Even the better off workers could not run to one so a carpet sweeper had to do the work. Mother had one of these which she pushed along the floor, but carpets themselves were rare. They were simply too expensive. Most floors had cold lino with just a few home-made rugs scattered about. There was very thin carpeting on the stairs and Mother had to brush this on her hands and knees. If there should be any kind of carpet every spring this had to be taken up, manhandled outside, hung on a strong line and beaten by hand. The dust which used to leave the carpet was enough to asphyxiate the carpet beater.

Homemade rugs were made from wool clippings in holes on a canvas or, if very poor, crude sacking was used and old rags and worn out clothes were cut into strips. These were incredibly hard wearing and warm to the feet but also dirt traps of the highest order. The upstairs only ever had lino which had to be mopped daily to remove the fluff. Some extra proud housewives would even get down and polish this and if they were foolish enough to put a little rug down a broken leg from a fall usually resulted.

All the bedrooms had coal-fired grates and chimneys which were never lit because of the sheer cost and hassle of carrying coal up the stairs and ashes back down. The consequence was the bedrooms were – freezing! We used to have cold, frosty and snowy winters then – certainly no hint of global warming. Each bed had a hot water bottle which warmed about 12 inches square while the rest of the bed was bitterly cold. Marvellous for later rheumatism but we thought nothing of it. Going to bed was just a trial and getting up could be even worse. We did not moan, we were all in the same boat So what was the point?

Wash day was terrible and always on a Monday because everyone wore clean clothes on the Sabbath. The housewife only washed once a week because it was such a trial. The clothes were sorted out on Sunday night, white in one container, coloured in another and woollens in the third. Early on Monday morning the fire was lit under the copper to boil the water; this might be in the scullery (kitchen) or an outhouse. Sometimes the kindling would be damp and it was hard work to get the fire going.

It took simply ages to boil water, into which the 'whites' went first, along with chopped up soap. This was then 'possed' with the hand gadget made from copper with a short wooden handle. When the whites were done they were rinsed and put to soak in a large container into which a tablet of Reckitt's blue had been dissolved. The rest of the laundry was dealt with in the same way and when rinsed the water had to be squeezed out with a mangle. This was very hard labour. Then the laundry had to be dried. If the weather was bad, clothes had to be dried anyway. Indoors were a multitude of strings from one end of the ceiling to the other. Finally came the last trying effort to iron the whole lot.

On wash days dinner was a rough and ready affair, simply cold meat left over from the Sunday joint and anything else an astute housewife had-to-hand. Even if there was a force eight blizzard raging Monday was still wash day. Tuesday was given over to cleaning one specific room and then other rooms in the week. No man needed a calendar if he knew his housewife's routine which never varied – come hell or high water. To my mother cleanliness most definitely stood next to godliness. There was a place for everything and woe befall a culprit if this order was not kept. That included me and my toys. They all had to be packed away smartly when I had finished playing with them and the books go back neatly in a bookcase father had made.

We had no bath, working families rarely did. What we did have was an enormous tin affair, kept hanging on the wall of an outhouse; this was brought in and tediously filled with hot water boiled in saucepans on the gas stove. I had the first bath and then my parents – all in the same water. Horrifying to us today but what else could we do when there were no public baths available?

We had one toilet – outside – so it was a case of chamber pots at night. Looking back to these days it was a crude way of living but we thought nothing of it because we were all in the same boat.

Mother's cooking skills were magnificent but Father was also very clever with those clumsy-looking hands of his. He repaired our shoes, saving cobbler's expenses. He hammered Blakey's on the toes and heels of my shoes, which I loved as they made a gorgeous noise and were perfect for sliding. He decorated our home using the best paint and paper he could afford. If anything in the home broke, he could usually repair it. He and Mother made a pretty fine team.

Girls' clothing then was horrible because they all had to wear a liberty bodice to keep out the cold and I hated being muffled in them. Bras were unheard of so female adults wore bust bodices, which must have had nil sex appeal. Knickers were always navy blue, with long legs. There were no Y fronts for males, just long-legged pants made from thick material and always white. Women most certainly did not wear slacks although they might get away with long-legged shorts in the warm weather if they had a bold nature. All boys wore grey short trousers which ended at the knees and long thick socks held up by elastic garters (which could be utilized as catapults). Boys did not wear long trousers until they started work at 14 years.

I was simply another average girl but I did excel at reading. Although very active I was prone to coughs and colds, which is hardly surprising with our cold and damp bedrooms. My parents were worried about these coughs because Grandpa Bullen had 'consumption' (tuberculosis). My mother was especially fearful, even though I had missed the usual children's diseases except measles and whooping cough.

I was dosed with cod liver oil, which I loved, and Scotts emulsion, which I hated. Mother persisted with the latter until I had been sick a few times when she received the message loud and clear. There was no NHS but my prudent parents belonged to the National Deposit Friendly Society, known as the NDFS. Each month a few shillings were paid into this, which covered the three of us. When I was four years old they took out a penny death policy. In the early 30s many children died before school age but this policy would have been enough to bury me as funeral expenses were dreaded.

Policy number 127745930 at one old penny a week was taken out on my life through the Prudential Assurance when my parents address was 66 Lindley Road, Leyton, London. My father continued this until his death, when I took over. By then we had become decimal and one pound covered five whole years until the Pru said I need not bother any more. This should make interesting reading for my executors when I pop my clogs!

One day my mother took me to see that awesome person – the Doctor. I can remember him examining me very carefully and listening to my chest before I was sent from the room. Shortly afterwards Mother reappeared and I could see she had been crying. The world stopped dead in its tracks. When she reached home she was closeted with my father for ages and when I saw him he was white-faced.

This was so unnatural I became worried and alarmed. What had I done? I learned much later that I had been diagnosed as having weak lungs. Before I could catch my breath or my wits I was packed off to a convalescent home in the depths of the country. I hated it. I missed the gang to start with, as well as Bo. I did not like any of the other children and they did not like me either. They were very poor children from slum homes, children who did not know what shoes were for and whose clothing was a hodgepodge of cobbled together rags. They had a lice, nits, spots and worse. They were narrow-chested, riddled with tuberculosis and had the bent legs of Ricketts. They knew that they were the no-hopers of their day, the outcasts, the dregs of society. They were also extremely tough, street-wise kids, which was why they were still alive. Their code of conduct was that of rats. Only the toughest survived. They were cruel, vicious, cheats and liars. They were just about beyond redemption although through no fault of their own.

Because my parents had their tiny little shop I was considered a 'toff' and fair game for all of them. Most of them were bigger than me and how cruel they were! I was pinched, punched, thumped and endured two weeks of hell with them. I tried to fight back but I was too small, weak and thin. They had no qualms at all about beating up a little girl and it was after this dreadful experience I made a solemn vow.

"One day," I told myself, gritting my teeth with pain and frustration, "one-day I'll be strong and no one – no one – will ever do this to me again. I will learn to fight properly and I will make sure I always win!"

I have very strenuously kept this vow and no one since then has ever beaten or walked over me. If my parents had known, all hell would have broken loose, especially from my small, feisty Mother. But it was too far for my parents to come and visit me and in my letters I said not a word. It was not done to tell tales to adults and I had been brought up to paddle my own canoe without complaint.

What were the staff doing to allow such a state of affairs? Why did they not stop the vicious treatment handed out to the small and weak? It was probably because they were overworked and underpaid as well as too few in numbers for proper supervision.

I was delighted to be home again with Bo and the gang. My parents were not so pleased because I greeted them with a huge attack of coughing. Then my mother bent over me and nearly threw a fit. My hair was covered with lice. She pounced upon my scalp as if she were a direct descendant of Geronimo. My hair was cut and my scalp attacked with Dettol and other foul concoctions. The invaders did not have a chance and this became a daily job for a week until they had all disappeared. My clothes were burned and I was scrubbed until my skin was sore.

Still, one good thing came out of all this – my mother vowed that I would never go to any such place again.

It was September 1939 and on the third of the month war was declared. I was 9½ years old but even at that tender age I had a suspicion that life was never going to be the same again. I was correct.

Chapter IV

Change came but slowly at first although the talk of war was everywhere at all times, even with the gang. In my childish naiveté it seemed boring. Then something quite astounding happened. There was no school. I went to a Church of England School because they gave a good all-round education, yet suddenly, out of the blue, all the schools were shut. The arrival of a visitor from Mars would have been less astounding than this one particular event.

The streets all around echoed with the talk of war and even the horrors of the last war from that generation. Personally, I thought war must be a wonderful thing if it was powerful enough to shut schools.

About this time I asked for a cycle and my parents produced a battered old sit-up-and-beg variety, I was soon off out and about exploring. This meant I did not see much of the gang and I realized I didn't mind. That I was growing and changing did not occur to me. I was glad to get away from home because now there were fierce rows and the atmosphere could be awful.

They were all over the shop. My father held that now we had officially gone to war, the shop should be sold. My mother said it should be kept instead and events proved her right. Shortly we were to be issued with ration books. The politicians had learned from World War I, when there was no official rationing and many people went without. This would not happen a second time, they vowed. All people, irrespective of their finances, would be entitled to a certain amount of food per week. Each housewife, holding the ration books for her family, was compelled to register them with a specific shop. No wandering around from one shop to another, bargain-hunting. Goods were delivered to the shop in question, just enough for the customers who had registered with it. This meant, of course, a guaranteed income for the shop. Many of these little corner shops, when war ended, found they were sitting on a very nice nest egg – all thanks to the rationing system. So by selling their shop my parents missed out on acquiring a very useful sum of money. Mother had an instinct and genuine acumen for business. My father did not. It was the old story again, the Wallis hesitancy. Father's decision was a height of stupidity and I do not think Mother ever forgave him because this was a second time in their marriage he had loused things up through lack of boldness.

In my father's defence, he was, at 39 years old, uncertain whether or not he would be called up into the armed services. Young men have always been the preferred age group for cannon fodder and Father thought he might be conscripted into active service. He was in the tail end of the call-up for World War I, though just missed fighting. He may have been worried about Mother coping alone but she would have done brilliantly. It was also tragic because the working classes are only ever given one chance in life. Miss it and it won't appear a second time.

The next curious event was the gas mask. Father appeared one day with one each, all packed into square cardboard boxes. He explained what they were and it was made clear to me that I was to wear mine if the siren sounded in a certain way. Now everything about war took on a very different aspect which I did not like.

"Where is Bo's?" I asked my father.

He exchanged a queer look with Mother, then knelt and explained to me that they did not issue them for pets.

I was utterly horrified. "Why not?" I blurted out, then started to think it through. Bo would die! She would go to heaven to be with Grandpa Wallis, so now, for the very first time, the meaning of what war meant hit me.

"I won't have it, do something Dad!" I looked at him with blind faith, knowing his clever hands.

He tried, oh how he tried, to pacify me. He spent hours trying to seal the stable doors and windows so Bo could be put in there, even though he had already made the decision we were going to leave. It certainly never entered my head that if the shop was to be sold and we went to live somewhere else there would not be a stable.

The next thing was my father started to give me complex and detailed instructions which soon filled my head. I was taught about planes and bombs and what the latter could do. No punches were pulled. My father explained all about the hazards of blast from a bomb and how windows must be left open so the blast could go through the house and not demolish the walls. He taught me how to use a stirrup pump against incendiary bombs as well as sand, buckets of which were placed in strategic positions.

Grandma Wallis still lived with us, with no sign of her going elsewhere now we were at war. She also took lessons and we practiced together working the stirrup pump. My very puny 10-year old arms and her wrinkled aged ones but father reckoned the pair of us acting in unison should be able to deal with one incendiary bomb if he and Mother were absent for some reason.

Finally I was rehearsed at night, in the dark, in getting dressed rapidly and when I undressed in the evening I was taught to place my clothes in strategic positions so they could be donned in a flash. I was so brainwashed that even now, as an old person, I still follow the same routine. Then I was taught a variety of knots so that escape from upstairs could be accomplished with bed sheets. By the time my father had finished I consider I must have been the best prepared child for war in the whole of that city.

"For the duration" became a phrase we were soon to know. Many schools were forced to go onto a part-time basis because so many buildings were incapable of being satisfactorily reinforced against bomb blasts. I suddenly found I had to attend a huge council school where I was soon lost in a mass of highly excited, milling youngsters. The timetable went to pieces and it must have been a dreadful time for the head and his teachers.

Mr Beaumont was the head and he really ruled with a rod of iron. He needed to as well. Circumstances dictated he be a strict disciplinarian and not hesitate to use his cane. He didn't either. The classes were large 40, 50 and even 60 children, because this school covered a huge catchment area. The head terrified me, so I never deviated from the straight and narrow. Even the gang members were very careful of what they did and when.

There were children in every nook and cranny. The assembly hall, after morning roll call and prayers, was divided into 'open air classes'. There were even small groups of pupils in broom cupboards from which the doors had been removed. It was utter bedlam and learning was just about impossible. Yet this head was a genius, I now realize. He must have worked extremely hard organizing. He brought back retired teachers. He found garden sheds and insisted nothing was going to be disrupted just because of a trifle like a war. We detested him.

He was a prowler. No class or cupboard was safe from his sudden entry and though not a big man in height he was built on the lines of a solid tank. He was generous with his praise. There was not one bit of trouble at that school while I was there by any pupil and it is only now, with maturity, I can appreciate what Mr Beaumont did. The educational standards were still high and eventually we started to learn a lot and received a pretty good, rounded education.

I used to feel so sorry for some boys because they came from a large orphanage and were the dregs of society. They wore the same short grey trousers and woollen socks but these were threadbare from countless washes. The trousers were always hand-me-downs, well patched and far from neat. Hair was close cropped against nits and lice. The boys had white, terrified and thin faces. They were all too frightened to say a word to anyone.

At least every child in the school had shoes, even if they were a paper thin and scruffy. Milk was available for all children and for those from poor families it was vital. Some of these children were half-starved and would faint at assembly. It was a shocking indictment of those times. If people refer to the 'good old days' they certainly never lived in them as the poor working class.

Years later I read a book by a Nazi who stated the British would be easy to thrash because their soldiers would be undernourished weeds. We all know how wrong he was about the thrashing bit, but the latter part of his statement was very correct. Service recruits had, by and large, to be fed up before they could be turned into fighting material. Every cloud does indeed have a silver lining and World War II, with rationing, gave everyone fair shares, so that when peace did come, those who returned vowed never to live as they had in the past – and good for them.

With the official rationing some children were able to eat a balanced diet for the first time in their lives. Once the poor families realized they were not going to be left out, as happened in World War I, it was amazing how money was found to buy food. But for those already riddled with tuberculosis and rickets, it was all too late.

All schools received medical inspections on a regular basis, which must have taken quite a bit of organizing. No one could opt out. We were all examined physically: teeth, eyes, ears, hair for nits, bodies and clothing. We were made to have injections whether our parents agreed or not. There was simply no arguing with officialdom and later statistics proved we became quite a healthy generation. Why did it take war to bring all this about?

By now, I was approaching that awesome period of life when I had to sit for The Scholarship. This was a great milestone in any child's life, far more so than today's similar examinations. Would we go to an important secondary school, a top one, or a mediocre one?

I was not intellectual like my mother, I knew that, but neither was I ultra-dim. Today I would be called a late developer. I did excel at writing compositions, now called essays. A harbinger of the future? I certainly could not be equalled for my reading ability. At sums, though, I was hopeless. No calculators then; all had to be worked out in the head or on paper.

There was dreadful determination as we sat for this examination. I knew I could not hope to get one so I was not bothered. This was during the phoney war period when we all dutifully carried our gas masks everywhere. We had been suitably indoctrinated into the various notes of the siren denoting either the Alert all the All Clear. Every window in every home in the land was hidden behind ugly blackout curtains. Now that rationing was in full force certain items disappeared for The Duration. Among these were bananas and ice cream.

The gang changed. The boys were growing up as families moved and tensions arose when the adult males were called up for military service. Quite a few adult females began to appear in uniform so, almost overnight, the old gang disintegrated. Street games also vanished. We were all waiting – for something.

I still had my coughs and colds, which rarely stopped me doing what I wanted, but my parents were still worried to death. Then came an incredibly savage winter, with severe frosts and much deep snow. Like most dogs, Bo adored revelling in snow and the pair of us had a marvellous time. The snow went on and on and life was grand again.

One day Mother took me aside when we were alone and, red-faced, spelled out the facts of life. Like all children I had listened to smut from the streets but even so I was rather astonished. It all seem very weird to me. I now guessed why father had taken the dog for a walk.

"It's time you had the facts!" Mother ended, with the relief at her embarrassment.

I didn't quite know what to say but then a thought struck me. All of a sudden, it was very crystal clear.

"Why is Uncle Bob adopted?" I dared to ask at last.

Mother was thunderstruck.

"How do you know?" she gasped.

I had to come clean then about the result of my snooping long ago. "So who is he?" I persisted.

Mother had been caught flat-footed and she never lied.

"He is your half-brother!" she said, and burst into tears.

Now it was my turn to be stunned into silence because Mother's distress was dreadful. The whole disgusting story came out. It was all Grandma Bullen's fault from start to finish. Although my mother was so intellectually bright that the school's inspector wanted her to go to university, Grandma scorned this. Mother was but a girl, unimportant and insignificant because she was incapable are going down the pit to hew coal like the men. Instead she was packed off down south to a very distant branch of the family to be their skivvy. She was not told any facts of life whatsoever and they had a hearty son. The inevitable happened and Mother was packed off back to Yorkshire again, in total disgrace. In a Methodist area, in those disgusting narrow-minded days, her shame and misery was enough to turn a weaker person mental. But my tough little Mother survived, said the equivalent of "to hell with the narrow-minded so and so's", then got on with her own life and made her first trip to Leicester to paddle her own canoe. The baby was adopted by Grandmother and, without the young father's consent, given his surname, which I will not mention here because I detest it for the cruel way they all treated my mother.

I hugged her (and we were not a tactile family) and suddenly realized I had grown up a bit, which was no bad thing. Mother never did wholly recover from the cruel, almost barbaric, treatment she received from this family. Is it any wonder I hate their name? I never thoroughly liked Grandmother Bullen after learning all this. All this suffering was unnecessary just because a young girl of 15 was incapable of slinging a pick down the pit to hew for coal. I also considered Grandpa Bullen extremely weak but it was only later I realized he was a slowly dying man.

We moved to 39 South Knighton Road into a rented semi-detached house. Father was now an air raid warden and due to go into the fire brigade for the Blitz raids which everyone knew were going to come. The house was rented out for the enormous sum of 14 shillings a week and it was three miles from the city centre, which meant I had to go to school by bus until the examination results were known.

I hated the thought of leaving my precious friends even though we were growing apart. I saw them all and we vowed eternal friendship and promised faithfully to keep in touch. A few weeks after the move I cycled back and they did not want to know me. Now that I lived in a semi I had moved up the class scale. We did have a tiny morsel of garden back and front so had become superior to West Avenue. I was a social outcast! It was a very valuable lesson to me in learning not to cling to the past but only to consider the future. I never did know what happened to the gang members – if they survived the war.

We moved on the first of April 1940 and I went to take Bo for a walk to explore while my parents unpacked and hung the blackout curtains. We had not gone a dozen paces when we met another little girl. She looked at me and then the dog.

"Does she bite?" was her first question.

"Oh yes!" I hastened to lie, to impress, because Bo was the most soft-hearted Alsatian one could ever hope to meet. But I was not going to tell this to a strange girl – at least not at this stage.

"I'm Ann Rawson!" she volunteered, and asked to know my name. And that's how we started a friendship which, at the time of typing this, is of 67 years duration. She lived five houses down from me and after meeting Ann, even though there were some boys in the street, I was no longer interested in anything as childish as a boy's gang! I didn't want males. I had my two best mates Bo and Ann. Even when I later travelled the world, Ann and I would soon pick up the threads of our friendship again. We might not see each other for a whole year but once we met the conversation carried on regardless.

That's what you call a real friendship.

Chapter V

Number 39 was totally different to our previous homes. It had quite large rooms with built-in wall cupboards which were normal then. Under the stairs was so large it was almost a room. Heating was by the inevitable coal fire and the kitchen was miniscule, nothing but a tiny scullery. Again there was no electricity but my father soon remedied that. There was the usual gripe from the electricity authority until they checked his work with amazement and again offered him a job with them but it was much too late. Even with a good coal fire in the main sitting room it was a very cold damp house. Father said there was something wrong with the damp course but we were at war and house repairs had all been put on hold 'for the duration'.

Ann and I spent a lot of time together in each other's homes and how I envied her a bathroom and indoors toilet. She lived with her grandmother in a freehold property and went to a school as a private pupil. No chamber pots for her! We had a moth-eaten piece of garden at the back about 10' x 4' and it was from this muddy patch of ghastly earth I became interested in planting seeds to grow food to eat. I was almost possessive over this patch of garden and understood at last why man will go to war to obtain territory.

Our lives had begun to change. Now all males of fighting age were called up and women without commitments had to go into directed labour if able-bodied. Because of my age and the fact Grandma Wallis still lived with us Mother had to go. Firstly she worked in the food office in the city centre but when her ability with figures was discovered she moved to the Midland bank, where she began as an ordinarily cashier and ended up as the head cashier.

Father was now in the fire service and they were all training hard for when the bombs would start to come. I went to school one day, thinking it was just another normal day, when the head told me I had won my scholarship.

I could not wait to get home because weeks ago Mother had promised me a 10-shilling note if I did obtain this. Incredible wealth! When she came back from work, tired out, I went to her and just said, "You owe me 10 shillings!"

My words made her day and for a few seconds she was stunned into silence. Then she opened her purse and passed the note to me. "Can I do what I like with it?" I asked nervously, remembering back to the days when I had been forced to save those two pennies.

"Yes!" she said proudly, "You can do what you like with it!"

Of course, as soon as I was given liberty to splurge the whole lot, I decided to save it instead. Kids can be very contrary. I coughed my delight because I was still plagued with a weak chest. I was also small and puny for my age. Then Mother made a suggestion. Whether from instinct or knowledge I had no idea. Less than half a mile away was the Kenwood swimming pool, open air with unheated water and quite large. She said she would buy a season ticket so I could go each day after school if I wanted to. It cost the horrendous sum of 15 shillings and gave entrance at all times without queuing. I loved the idea, even though I didn't know how to swim. The pool opened from 1st May until the last day of October and how I took to the water! I was soon swimming, even when the water was bitterly cold.

And I began to thrive. The coughs and colds disappeared and I began to grow in leaps and bounds. Oddly enough, Johnny Weissmuller, the star who acted as Tarzan, was also a weak, sickly boy until he took up swimming in the open air. He grew into a large and very powerful man.

The next very thrilling event was when Ann told me she could learn to start pony riding at a school about 5 miles away. The cost though was five shillings an hour, a tremendous sum. I begged and pleaded and kept on and on because I was so desperate to learn how to ride. It is weird to think this childhood yearning would take me down a path so unfamiliar to all members of our family.

Eventually both of my parents agreed and I guess they were so delighted with my improved health I was encouraged to spend as much time as possible outdoors doing something quite physical. I cycled the 5 miles to the riding school, produced my five shillings and stated bluntly, "I want to learn how to ride!"

I had arrived too late for the usual lessons but was put on the back of an old ex-racehorse and walked down the lane. I was hooked! It was tremendous and the saddle so natural. The lady talked nothing but horses and I drank it all in.

I soon left Ann far behind because she lacked my drive and had a breathing problem not helped by horse dust. Eventually she was forced to stop medically.

I cycled, rode and swam. I grew and grew. My frame took on good muscle and my complexion changed from the sallow to rosy. I bristled with health and vitality and my parents were delighted.

The next event was selecting a higher school. All four of the girls' schools in the city were choosy in accepting their pupils. My parents picked one which had an excellent academic record for producing teachers. It was not my choice the children called it 'the school for snobs'. I did not want that label but I need not have worried. The interview was a fiasco. I was sat in the room, facing the wall and told to draw a plan with the furniture positioned. I didn't even know what a plan was! So that was instant rejection.

The next on the list was the Alderman Newton's Girls' School which was my preference because their sports record was brilliant. Their headteacher was Miss Davies, who had been brought back from retirement 'for the duration'. How different was this interview. She asked me what I like to read. Instead of talking about the usual comics, *Beano, Dandy* and *Hotspur* I was instantly well away, happy to discuss my favourite books. Jack London's *Call of the Wild* and *White Fang* as well as all of Zane Grey's books. I think that dear old lady had the shock of her life about these works and I stated my dislike of Dickens in general. We ended up having a very educated conversation which certainly impressed her and gave me instant selection. Mother was so proud of me. I was going to get what had been denied to her. Poor Mother. It was a good job she did not know in advance and as well that father was very laid-back about the whole affair.

Our uniform was bottle green and very smart too. Because both of my parents were now working, even though it was a state school, they had to pay three guineas a term for me. If for any reason I left early there would be a penalty payment of 15 guineas. This was a disgraceful means test.

It did not take me long to realize it was all a ghastly mistake. The school was certainly very academic but I was shaken at the methods employed. It was all rigid cramming and I was only interested in sport, writing, reading and horse riding at the weekends. There was also the very disruptive experience of the war itself plus the fact I would turn into a late developer though no one knew this at the time, self included.

My morale began to sink. I was acutely aware of the cost of this education plus my parents delight but I started to become very unhappy. I was superb at reading, writing and sport but algebra, geometry and trigonometry were quite beyond me and I began to dread these particular lessons, even history and geography were different to the previous school so they too would too left me cold. I was totally unsuited to this type of education but dare not say a word at home.

We were loaded with homework all of which was a personal night mare and it was obviously too much for any child whose days and nights were regularly interrupted with the wail of sirens, the noise of the ack-ack guns to say nothing of bombs being dropped. In was much worse for the older girls trying to study for their school certificates and matriculation examinations. Many of them failed which was hardly surprising when one considers the conditions under which we were supposed to learn.

Many children were evacuated from the cities to the countryside and even to Canada. My parents asked me if I would like to go to Canada. I was utterly horrified. That would be running away from the ogre called Hitler, sheer cowardice. One girl in my form did take up this offer and we made her life a misery for this decision because children can be very cruel. I think she was heartily glad to go in the end.

Now and again Bob used to come to have a little holiday with us. He worked underground at Wath main colliery which he entered at 14 years. I viewed him with different eyes but never let on I knew about our relationship though I expect Mother told him. The trouble was the age gulf. He was 10 years older than me. A man while I was still nothing but a child. We got on fairly well even though he did insist on calling me "Teapot!" It would take maturity for us to find a rapport and how much alike we really were. Bob was all right in my child's eyes.

We learned to live with the war although the bombing had turned into blitzs which were horrendous in London and other cities. Even small Bath was attacked under the German Baedeker plans and Bristol was savaged from the bombers.

Days appeared to vanish in oblivion; it seemed there had always been war. Peace was forgotten. Certain foods vanished 'for the duration' even sweets and chocolates which must have been very good for our teeth. Our merchant Navy had to run the gauntlet of the dreaded a U-boat packs and in those early years of the war it was our ships which were losing. So many incredibly brave men died at sea, especially those who sailed the tankers. Being burned alive was apparently inevitable but a risk accepted by those sailors.

As certain foods vanished other weird concoctions appeared. Recipes invented by the Ministry of Food used that which was available. Potato cakes and dried or powdered eggs were two, plus the iniquitous margarine, known as 'Maggie-Ann'. I have never cared for margarine since the end of the war and never will, even though it was all so long ago. Corned beef was another highly dubious food and though it is all right in the 21st century eyes I still view it with disdain. At one time the butter ration per person was 2 ounces a week. The housewife could take extra sugar instead of jam which Mother always did for her home baking and preserving. Everyone was encouraged to drink tea without sugar. I have not done so from that day to this. I am sure my dentist approves!

Strangely enough, we all fared rather well on these rations, with better figures, except for the more corpulent wide boys, known as 'spivs', but at least no one went hungry this time round. Children even became rosy cheeked, filled with energy, glowing with health and vitality. Looking back this was a bonus of war.

At school we were encouraged to go out into the countryside and gather the natural produce of the fields and hedges. Young nettle leaves boiled lightly were very good. Rose hips would be turned into a delicious syrup and in the autumn there were nuts which we dried and saved for Christmas. Dry sticks were perfect for lighting fires so nothing was wasted. What the farmers could not gather in the townies did.

Excursions were still cheap and people were encouraged to try and get away and have a break. The trains were always jam packed with service personnel going from here to there. Coach travel was in its infancy but also there was a shortage of petrol. What those brave tanker men brought in was reserved for the military. Many cars were put on blocks and raised off the ground 'for the duration'. Those with cycles looked after them very carefully because tyre replacements were just about impossible to obtain. What rubber which came into the country was again for the military.

Train travelling in wartime was a unique form of hell for all concerned. The locomotives had to pull extra-long trains using inferior coal, so speed did not come into it. There would be long delays for passenger trains, which were often shunted onto sidings while more important troop and ammunition trains were given priority. A traveller arrived 'sometime'. The journey of a couple of hours in peacetime could take all day and even half the night if there was a raid further up the line. To get a seat was a work of art. Service personnel with huge kitbags and sailors with rolled-up hammocks took up so much space. Often the luggage racks above the seats would contain weary servicemen, sound asleep. The toilets would also have many in them sleeping. The aisles were solid with bodies and it was a case of push and shove with few manners in use. Yet everyone was so good-tempered about it all. Grumbles and groans were aimed at Adolf Hitler. We were all prepared to put up with this situation 'for the duration'.

When Ann was not available for playing I would wander off with Bo, not a very happy little girl with school hanging over me like the Sword of Damocles. I was never bored with my own company because life was too interesting. There was so much to see and do. I had been sternly warned not talk to strange men and certainly not to be enticed with a bar of chocolate. One day a soldier did try this on and I turned on my heels and bolted.

Trains were trains then – huge man-made monsters with their own distinctive sounds and smells, throbbing and grumbling with power as they belched steam from here, there and everywhere. When a long-distance train came into the station a man would walk along the track checking the wheels with a special hammer on the end of a long shaft. He was the official Wheel Tapper and I would follow his progress with great interest because his hammer made a specific sound, once heard never forgotten. I always waited anxiously for him to fault a wheel but I never did see this.

I spent many hours on the LMS platform, jotting down engine serial numbers, which had become the current child's craze, so I learnt quite a bit about locomotives and how to identify them from their wheels. At the same time I saw many distressing sights of soldiers, sailors and airmen with their female counterparts, couples being split up to meet who knew when, or if ever, again. The red caps – military police – everyone in uniform and carrying big gas masks, wives in husband's arms, children crying as well. Many women struggled to be brave until the train had pulled away, then they would go to pieces. War is so utterly stupid. There is no glamour attached to it whatsoever.

People helped one another then because we were all in the same situation. They would talk to strangers, there was a camaraderie brought about by shared hardship in danger. As a nation we pulled as one. Perhaps Hitler and his spies, because they were around, they had been slipped into the country in advance, never wholly expected this. Once threatened there was no north and south, east or west, just a people and one nation fighting to retain the God given freedom which was their right from birth.

Dunkirk came and went, our most brilliant defeat, when all the little ships, even tiny launches and yachts, sailed over the Channel to rescue 'our boys' stranded on the beaches of

France. Over a quarter of a million were saved, so defeat was turned into a glorious victory against adversity.

Songs were produced which became enormous favourites such as *The White Cliffs of Dover* and oddly enough the German *Lily Marlene*. Everyone listened to the BBC for the latest news updates and events at home were always geared around the next news bulletin's time.

Newspapers were very small as paper was rationed. Books came out printed on ghastly paper which would never have seen the light of day pre-war. Clothes were mended, patched and patched again until we all looked shabbily the same. Only service personnel were considered smart but we did not give a damn; nothing could dampen our spirit.

The German Luftwaffe continued to blitz our cities with the intention of breaking us. Poor London was hammered night after night and the East End, with the docks, suffered terribly. Traders whose shops were bombed in the night would shrug their shoulders and carry on the next morning on the open pavement.

The National Fire service came into its own with a vengeance. My father was stationed less than half a mile from home on the basis of 48 hours on and 24 off unless there was a raid. Once these started in our area we never knew when we would see him again. A system was developed which became a godsend. As one city received its nightly destroyers the next city or town down the line would send reinforcements in a convoy. And so it would go on, up and down the country. It was a complicated system from the logistics point of view but it worked beautifully. Thanks to our early invention of radar we were able to track the bombers' approach and get some idea which place was the intended target and get a convoy moving with reinforcements. If more than one lot of bombers came over to attack two targets this system came under stress but it still worked.

My father had always had a love affair with the motorcycle and he was selected to be a dispatch rider, known as a Don R, to escort fire convoys. There were always two. One would ride at the front as a pathfinder, the other at the rear. They would interchange periodically to make sure they hadn't lost a fire appliance. It was always in the pitch dark in the blackout and each motorcycle headlight was reduced to a mere strip of illumination through a headlamp grill so unless really tailgating it was easy for an appliance to go charging off in the wrong direction. These convoys moved at top speed. In the built-up areas there were the hazards and detritus of war like unexploded bombs, crater holes and collapsed buildings all jumbled up with burned out vehicles like buses and trams. It was a very hazardous occupation.

My father rode a 1,000cc Indian motorcycle which he always said was difficult to handle as it had a foot gear change, foot brake and foot clutch. Father swore that the bike rider needed three feet, especially at a standstill with the engine running. There were no simple batteries for starting, it was a kick-start and that big engine caused many a broken ankle when other men tried to use it.

Father had some hair-raising experiences on that bike in the blackout. It was pretty scary to ride such a powerful bike in the pitch dark at top speed with a huge fire appliance directly behind the back wheel. One dark winter night, Father was going flat out, leading a convoy, when he hit black ice. As it happened, it was on a long stretch of country road. The next thing he knew was that he and his bike went into a violent skid, the bike soared over the hedge into a ploughed field and landed right way up with father still astride. It all happened so fast that the convoy carried on in blissful ignorance that it had just lost one Don-R!

He also had quite a number of spills, as did all the Don-Rs, some of whom were killed or maimed for life with horrific injuries. Coventry, like Birmingham, had often been bombed, but one day the traitor William Joyce – who we all called Lord Haw-Haw – broadcast that the next night Coventry would be obliterated. He was an Irishman but made the crass mistake of holding a British passport. After the war we captured and tried him and he was executed for treason. Proper thing too.

Leicester is about 20 miles from Coventry as the crow flies and I remember well Mother, myself and Grandma looking up at the sky where, in the direction of Coventry, there was a horrible vivid glow as the Luftwaffe tried to satisfy Lord Haw Haw. We had no idea where Father was but guessed he had taken a convoy from Leicester to Coventry. We did not see him for many days. When he did eventually come home, he was red-eyed, utterly exhausted, filthy dirty and he stank to high heaven. An unpleasant smell, which I now realize came from dead bodies. He had indeed taken a relief convoy to Coventry and stayed on. To the day he died he would never discuss this time, so we all gave up asking.

Many decades later my husband was reading a non-fiction book about the war called *Unsung Heroines,* published by Sedgwick and Jackson in 1990. He called me over.

"Know anyone?" he asked me.

I took the book and studied the large photograph of the WVS collecting water from a bowser to make tea for the men struggling to deal with the aftermath of a raid. And there, in his Don-R gear, was my father. He had the ability to smell a cup of tea from a mile away and there he stood, in the photograph on page 61, hopefully waiting for a brew up. I wanted to buy the book but could not get a copy, so had to use a photocopier. It was all very astonishing.

So far Leicester had only been lightly touched, with just a few sneak raids, then that swine Lord Haws Haw broadcast on "Germany Calling!" that we were next on the list for decimation. He wasn't joking either.

That particular night I was in the house alone with deaf grandma and Bo. Father was goodness knows where and Mother was working late at the bank, where they were involved in a mysterious occupation known as 'balancing the books'. When the siren sounded I followed father's instructions to the letter. I opened the doors and windows so the blast could travel through, made sure the buckets of water and sand were to hand with the stirrup pump available and then the three of us retreated under the stairs. Father had organized a small settee there and a chair with emergency water and food. I was 11 years of age and strangely not in the least frightened, obviously a result of my father's very sensible lessons.

The sirens finished their wailing warning note, which even today sends tingles down my scalp, and the raid started. This was no stray bomber but the real thing. Bombs started to rain down and their whining managed to penetrate even Grandma's deaf ears. Then there were the most thundering explosions and vibrations, which gradually came nearer and nearer. The noise was out of this world and cannot be described. A person has to live through such to understand. All German planes had a distinctive throbbing note to their engines, totally at odds to the sounds of the RAF planes. On top of all this there was the fiendish noise of our anti-aircraft barrage with many clangs on the roof has shrapnel and other objectionable items landed.

I was scared for my parents but there was nothing I could do. Ordinary people did not have telephones at home then. Very gradually the Luftwaffe moved away from our part of Leicester.

Quite a while later, Mother staggered in. She was white faced, utterly filthy and totally exhausted as she told her tale.

Leicester had been plastered with the incendiary bombs and then came the high explosives. All bank staff were escorted to an underground shelter where the vault was sited. Mother did not like this. She started to become agitated and when a Warden told her the raid had moved away from the centre and appeared to be heading south in our direction, she began to bubble and fizz. When Mother was like this, we had all learned to leave her very much alone.

At midnight she could stand it no longer and refused to stay. Short of tying her up, there was nothing the bank manager could do. Mother stormed outside among the raid's stench and collapsed buildings. She had 3 miles to walk home in the pitch dark, dodging bomb craters, collapsed buildings and others falling down. It was a ghastly experience but there were also screams from those trapped in the buildings. Bomb craters still smouldered and the police, firemen and Wardens worked frantically.

Mother ignored them all, her mind set on one thing only. Was number 39 still standing? She struggled on, stumbling, nearly twisted her ankle but headed remorselessly homewards. The Bullen temper really began to rise against Adolf Hitler. After only a little while the main road was blocked and she was halted by the police.

"You can't go any further Missus. We have an unexploded bomb just up there and it is a biggie!"

My highly stressed Mother eyed him, jaw set hard.

"I'm not walking around. It's much too far!" she told him acidly.

"But Missus, you simply can't go on," the unfortunate policeman insisted.

"Officer, you can take your stupid bomb..."

"It ain't my bomb, it's..."

But Mother had gone. She stormed past that bomb lying in the bottom of a huge crater, all five foot nothing of Yorkshire spitball and fury. Later on when the family discussed it the general consensus was the bomb in question would not have dared to explode as she passed by, stumbling through shards of glass and rubble.

The finale of this little tale is that the bomb was very alive indeed and the brave men of the unexploded bomb detachment had to spend quite some time making it safe because it was booby-trapped.

Chapter VI

Mother tried to see her side of the family as often as possible but travel was so difficult for them that she decided to go there instead and took me with her. I cannot remember much about the first journey, except that it took many hours to go less than 200 miles. Sheffield had been badly bombed so there were diversions and when we did reach Wath Main there was a huge queue for a rare bus.

It hit me that Yorkshire was totally different from Leicester, almost like another country. For a start no one spoke like me. I said 'grass' to rhyme with 'farce' but they pronounced it to rhyme with 'gas'. They all talked just like Bob and used a lot of dialect in their conversation. Initially I found it hard to understand anything they were saying. Yorkshire people call a spade a spade and not a shovel. If they like you, that's fine, but God help a person they don't like. I came to love the Yorkshire tykes because they are the real salt of this earth.

Grandma Bullen was born a Paskel and was one of umpteen children. Her parents' forebears came from a moneyed family who had connections with the brass and copper industry. James Paskel eloped with his bride to get work in the pit so it is to be figured out the family were against this involvement and they disowned him. Grandma Emma married Daniel Bullen and it was a shotgun wedding which makes her treatment of my mother even more disgraceful. Danny's father came from Norfolk farming stock and there was a heavy drink problem in that side. This may have been what made Grandma so hostile to alcohol.

Grandpa Bullen was 6'4" tall and a twin though his sibling died at birth. Grandma was 5 feet nothing. I once said to Bob she had been cruel to our Mother. He quickly replied she was cruel to all of them yet so religious.

Grandpa had been a marine in World War I and fought in the dreadful Gallipoli campaign and the Dardanelles. On 14th July 1915 Daniel Bullen of the Drake Battalion "behaved in a gallant and courageous manner at Achi Baba". Cold words but the story was different. He really should have had the Victoria Cross because three times Danny went back into no man's land and each time returned carrying a wounded officer. This was under fire. His commanding officer stated his name would go forward for a VC but before this could happen the CO was killed by a shell, so Danny received the next medal down for a ranker.

The three grateful officers clubbed together and bought him a handsome full Hunter watch and their names were inscribed on the back. But there is a sad end to this tale. After the war grandpa fell upon hard times. He was no longer able to work at the pit as a colliery rope splicer and he had also started to have trouble with his lungs. As they had a large garden in their rented home, Grandpa decided to go in for poultry to help the finances. My father lent what money he could to set him up but Grandpa was proud and independent. He insisted father take the watch as security for the loan. My father was very reluctant but did not want to get into a family row.

At this time my parents were newlyweds and lived in a tiny flat attached to a house called Hazel Dean, near Worthing, a house after which I am named. It was a rich man's house and one night burglars struck and ransacked the whole place when my parents were out. Grandpa's gold watch, although well hidden, was found and stolen. My parents were distraught, especially my father. On the back was Grandpa's full name and somewhere that brave man's watch is held by someone who has no right to it. I can never pass a pawnbroker without looking in the window on the off-chance the watch is there.

In Wath pubs proliferated, two and sometimes even three to a street, and they all did a roaring trade. Not because the men were raving boozers but because they worked down a hot and very dusty coal mine. The first pint of beer would vanish in a twinkling. The second eased the dust away while the third was to be savoured. Although a very strict Methodist area the church was on a hiding to nothing trying to stop the miners from drinking.

This house had a certain smell about it which I found wonderful. It was smell of freshly-baked bread and at this Grandma excelled. Outside there was another smell, encountered as soon as you stepped off the train. It was the smell of gases being burned off by the coalmine.

Grandma was not a brilliant fancy cook like my mother, and she would admit this, but her bread was outstanding. All her cooking was done on a range in the family room, behind which was a back boiler for constant hot water. I did not like her food because it was much too salty for my palate, necessary though for the miners who did so much sweating underground. She detested housework but was nevertheless spotlessly clean to a fault.

The downstairs of the house held the bathroom and toilet, the usual scullery and an outhouse adjoining. The family room was very large and here Grandpa had to have his bed. He had reached the stage where his slowly rotting lungs did not allow him to climb stairs. I learned he had been a very wild young man. He was quite an expert at playing the banjo yet all I can really remember of him is lying on his bed, spitting up blood. He died after the war with as much dignity as one can hope for with rotting lungs.

I realized he doted on my mother, so why hadn't he saved her from the miserable humiliations and dictatorial conduct of Grandma when my mother went through her terrible time? It was probably the onset of the tuberculosis. Mother's elder brother fancied a certain girl but Grandma put the mockers on that situation. Only Arthur, Mother's younger brother, was able to get away with murder, though even he eventually settled down. I liked him very much. Why do most people who are short have to make up their lack of inches by sheer bloody-mindedness?

I had problems with the children up there. They viewed me askance because I did not speak like them. I was a foreigner! Eventually I did make a couple of friends but played mostly with a cousin. 'The Hump' was the name for the railway sidings, which at that time formed the largest marshalling yard in the world after Chicago. The Hump also served two pits, the LMS railway as well as the LNER. When the wind was in a certain direction we heard the constant bangs and clangs as the wagons were shunted on the Hump to make up the goods trains.

Very near was a canal, no longer used but full of small fish like a minnows and sticklebacks. I and my cousin spent hours there trying to catch the fish; without much success but having great fun.

Wath Main colliery dominated the region with one of the largest slag heaps I have ever seen – and I have viewed a few in my time. It made a festering blot on the landscape and, like cancer, it grew more each year. At the same time the land of the area was sinking through subsidence caused by the removal of the coal below. Each time I went up there the vista was different as the village sank and the slag heap grew. The slagheap was out of bounds to all children and on this issue we did as we were told. We all came from miners' families and we had been brought up with danger. A slag heap looks firm but this is very deceptive and underneath there could be fire from internal combustion. Only a madman would try to walk on top of a slag heap.

We used to trespass on the Hump, even darting between the wheels of wagons which were getting ready to roll in our own stupid version of 'chicken'. We were fairly safe on the banks of the canal because we could all swim. Now, in this 21st-century, everything has gone – marshalling yards, slag heap and the canal – even the pit is no more. All the head and winding gear have been removed and the shafts concreted over. I still think it is a pity the canal was allowed to vanish because many firms could transport their goods that way instead of clattering up the road. I believe it is called progress though, isn't it?

Meals were different with Grandma Bullen and I did not like this either. It was not just her over salting fetish but the fact she served the Yorkshire pudding first, by itself, a hangover from the bad old days when it was critical to fill bellies as quickly as possible because there was little to come afterwards. There was also the horror of learning she did not believe in producing a pudding. Yet on the rare times when she came to Leicester to stay with us she had no trouble tucking into my mother's. Many decades later, when we stayed with my husband's family at York, I discovered no pudding was provided there! In my usual forthright way I sat with spoon and fork and asked bluntly, "Where's the pudding then?" Consternation! Especially as they always tucked into my puddings when they visited us. I like a pudding – I am my father's daughter that way.

Children are fairly adaptable animals because when I returned to Leicester I put all the Yorkshire ways aside not to be taken out again until the next visit.

The war dragged on and peace became a forgotten word. Everyone was expected to dig for victory. Famous old, posh lawns and wonderful flowerbeds were all dug up and filled with produce to eat. Food itself was never wasted because it was simply too precious. All scraps went into a smelly bucket for pigs which was collected twice a week on a regular basis. Waste was not allowed to exist.

Children grow up quickly in wartime, they have to. Bo had started to age. Her muzzle had gone white and she could only go for a short, slow walk now. Her devotion to me was as ardent as ever and this was reciprocated in full. One day father found a lump in her belly and took her to the vet for a consultation. I did not think much of this at the time but when he returned home without her I was shattered.

"Where is Bo?" I asked nervously.

He gave it to me straight. "She had cancer. She has been put to sleep It was the only kind of thing to do."

I was utterly devastated. I burst into a flood of tears which promptly set my parents off as well. Bo had been with us so long. She was part of the family. I could not believe I had lost my best friend. I was in a dreadful state for days because home was not the same. I have had many pets since and get horribly attached to have them even with their short lives and have to go through another painful goodbye. Only genuine animal lovers can hope to understand.

I was now very unhappy at school and my report said it all. "Could do better," was on all of them. My parents, especially my mother, were very distressed. But the trouble was I was *not* my mother. Academic learning at this stage was not for me. Most children then could only think of the time when they were 18 years and could join the services. All I could consider was being 14 years, leaving school and going out to work. All of which did not make the nicest atmosphere in the house.

The raids upon Leicester diminished and the next thing was a major invasion by American troops in the build up to D-Day and the invasion of Europe. I went riding every Saturday morning and was often whistled at by these strangers so I soon learned how to ignore them. On the way to the stables I also had to pass a large prisoner of war camp full of captured Germans or Italians. I was curious about the enemy and certain trusted men were allowed out to work on the local farms. I became adept at ignoring the whistles of the prisoners behind the barbed wire fences. They were obviously bored stiff, wondering what was happening to their families and glad of any sight to break the monotony of the day, even if it was just a young girl wearing jodhpurs, obviously going out riding.

Many of our villages, as we knew them, disappeared, as well as much of our countryside, under swathes of concrete for aircraft runways. We all became quite used to seeing armadas of planes towing gliders. Tanks would grumble down our roads. There was a subdued atmosphere among the civilian population. It was only too obvious that many loved ones would soon have to die.

Father had been transferred to the Immingham docks near to Grimsby, where the American liberty ships came in. The Americans have always been a very generous race and father waxed fat on their goodies and when he came home on leave, so did we.

My father had always been one of the world's heaviest smokers and no, he did not die of lung cancer, or even have it. He had now discovered a wonderful source of Lucky Strike cigarettes. The great problem for him and his mates was to get them out of the docks and past the dreaded Customs. The latter considered they knew every trick in the book but the British male can be very canny when he sets his mind to a problem!

The firemen put their heads together because they had just 'acquired' a huge consignment of cigarettes, tobacco, silk stockings, chocolate and alcohol. Declare this to the Customs? No way! They hit upon a solution but knew they could try it once and only once.

They spent a lot of time on their bright red fire engine until it was stuffed with contraband, hidden in the tyres, hoses and chassis, as well as on their bodies. An off duty bound man cycled blithely through Customs and, of course, he was 'clean'. He found a telephone and sent a frantic, panic stricken call for help that his house was on fire! Father and his mates kept their fingers crossed the Grimsby appliance would be engaged elsewhere, which it was. The Immingham appliance was scrambled into quick action and soon the very large Ack-Emma, complete with turntable and long ladders, was hurtling down the road. They shot past the Customs post, as was their right, while each man had a grave and serious expression on his face. The Customs had the gate open and ready for this emergency and thus one large fire appliance, stuffed with contraband, shot through with its bell clanging wildly. All they had to do then was drive to some deserted place and divide up their goodies.

Mother's birthday was on 6th June and that was also D-Day. I was 14 years and one month old and like the rest of the population, glued to the radio set. This was it!

I was now at the legal age to leave school and go out to work. I was just so miserable I couldn't leave the school quick enough. My mother was furious and it was about then a barrier arose between us. She would have to pay the 15 guineas penalty so she had reason to me mad with me, as well as the fact I was turning down all that which had been denied to her.

All I wanted to do was work with horses. All of the teen age years are difficult and I must have been a horrible problem to them. The rows became huge. The idea of working with horses was too stupid to contemplate. Females did not do such work. It was not even – nice! So she found me an office job shuffling bits of paper around one which was every bit as bad as school. I didn't last there long. So I was found another job as an office junior but one in which I learned how to operate a switchboard. I found this dead simple but I still wanted to work with horses. I was not sacked again but the manager had Mother in and tactfully said I was not really suited for being indoors.

She nearly went ape with fury but I stuck to my guns though it was very difficult. We clashed violently and ended up not liking each other very much.

"I want to work with horses!" was my battle cry.

"I'll put you in a factory!" Mother threatened.

"I'll get myself sacked again!" I warned her, and meant it.

"I'll take you before the magistrates as being beyond control!" was her retort.

"Then I'll just tell them I want to work with horses and you won't let me!"

Stalemate! Father very wisely left us to fight it out. The rows went on and on when Mother suddenly saw sense and capitulated. I think she was worn out with it all. Even the war had to go on the sidelines while this domestic battle took place. So Mother started looking for jobs for me when she did know the first thing about the subject. I was turned down here, I was turned down there, through my age and general inexperience. One place had racehorses and they put me on a fit animal and I was thrown off straight away and landed on the back of my head. Nobody wore helmets then. Such were for cissies.

I was offered a position that lasted less a week. I had violent headaches and started vomiting a lot. Quite obviously I had concussion but I was fit and strong and eventually put it all behind me. I went for an interview in Lincolnshire at a little village called Great Limber, which specifically requested a young girl to bring on. Miss Stops hesitated about offering me provisional employment because I was so young still. One thing clinched the job. She had hereditary deafness and all my life I had been used to dealing with deaf Grandma Wallis. So the job became mine at the sum of 15 shillings a week until Christmas, when this would go to a pound a week if I were satisfactory. I was to lodge in one of the cottages and she would pay my board.

So at last, I had my way and became happy. I could not have had a better person than Miss Stops to educate me in the equestrian world. Her standards were every bit as high as those of a top racing stable and ever after became my benchmark. I never had the slightest trouble in communicating with her because I could scribble rapidly and always had a pencil and notebook.

I started work at six in the morning, except when it was a hunting day, when it would be earlier. I worked until five in the evening but on a hunting day it could be eight or even nine o'clock at night. We stopped for breakfast at nine and took a half-hour lunch.

The work was sheer, hard physical labour but I thrived. At last I was doing something worthwhile. The village did not have electricity so the horses had to be clipped with a manual machine and my job was to turn the handle for over an hour. Is it any wonder I developed powerful arms? I became stronger and fitter and learned more each day and I was so happy.

Miss Stops rode side-saddle so this was more learning and I soaked it all up. I had no idea then that this knowledge and these experiences would be put to a very different use in a few decades' time. I did not think ahead, I was just supremely content for the day. I did not go out in the evenings. There was nowhere to go and I didn't have any money anyhow. Although on my precious afternoon off I had enough money to catch the bus to go into Grimsby and explore on foot.

The one bad spot concerned my digs. Rationing was still in force and it was even worse than during the war because it now encompassed bread and potatoes. My landlady had my ration book, as was her right, but she simply didn't feed me, obviously trying to make as much profit as possible from having me there.

I was constantly hungry, morning, noon and night. It was useless asking for more food because she didn't give it and I began to detest her. I said nothing to my employer because there was nowhere else to go. The chocolate ration then was one two ounce bar per week. In desperation I tried to eat the horses' food. I even went out in my lunch hour to look for nuts the squirrels might have hidden. I became incredibly thin but still said nothing to anyone.

When I went into Grimsby on my afternoon off I made straight for the market just to look at everything which could be eaten. When a stallholder turned his head I grabbed and bolted. I didn't care what it was as long as I could eat it and I don't care now if people know that I was then a thief. Before they condemn me they should try being hungry for week after week while doing physical labour.

I never said anything at home, of course. That would have been imprudent. The horses were at livery and the various owners would call in regularly, even when they weren't riding. One of them, somehow and from somewhere, produced a huge drum of black molasses to be given to the horses. I started on it first and it was this that kept me going and nothing else.

My little box bedroom was tiny and icy. The walls and ceilings were black with damp and I didn't know what a dry bed was either. It was a pretty grim six months I spent there and those days have never been forgotten either.

I went home to a precious days at Christmas and never stopped eating. I had always had a healthy appetite but this now went over the top. I never told my mother about the way I was being treated until many years later. She would have taken me away from my job and it would have been back to offices again. Also, I had been brought up not to complain but to get on with it, which I did. I did make a personal vow, which I have always kept, that when I was an adult, no visitor would ever leave my home feeling hungry.

Spring came and the horses were all roughed off to be in the fields. I went back to Leicester and did odd horse jobs in stables, which did not now meet my criteria of excellence, one of which was to take two horses from Leicester to Skegness in a railway horsebox. We did quite well until we reached a certain point where we were shunted onto a siding. I waited and waited and nothing happened so in the end I got out and, dodging trains, stormed into a nearby signal box. The signalman went to roar at me but I got in first and complained bitterly. He went very quiet and rather white, then admitted the horsebox had been forgotten.

So much for the railway. Later on in life I was to have another experience regarding an animal being forgotten by the railway. I have never trusted them since.

By the time the horses and I did eventually reach Skegness the owner was in rather a state, to put it mildly. I doubt he would ever trust the railways again either.

Then in the next autumn Miss Stops asked me to go back again until the following spring, which I agreed to on the understanding I would not live in that cottage with those people. When I explained why she told me I had been a silly girl for not putting her in the picture. This time I lodged at the inn with her. I spent a good winter there but in the spring I decided to go back to Leicester where, with my increased knowledge and expertise, I would try to obtain employment with horses in that region.

And that's exactly what I did.

Chapter VII

My new job was a place six miles away who kept many horses for hunting and breeding, along with working horses – 'carthorses', as they were called – for farm work in the summer. I did not mind this at all because it was an aspect of equestrian life about which I was ignorant.

At the same time I found out that there was a judo club in Leicester and I hastened to join. I had never forgotten those two dreadful weeks when I was beaten up in that convalescent home. I lived at home but was hardly ever there as is the wont with teenagers. The hours as usual were long then I would dash home and be off to the judo club.

Initially that was another fiasco. Before I could learn how to fight I had to know how to break my fall when being thrown. All I managed to do was hurt myself and I became despondent. One of the boys who had been watching my futile attempts grinned at me.

"I bet I know what's wrong," he said. "You are left-handed!"

I was astounded because I am right-handed but the black belt teacher nodded thoughtfully. "Left handers are rare in judo but try breaking your fall, especially the head roll, by leading with your left hand."

I did this and, eureka, that was the answer to the problem. I became a left-handed judoka and never once looked back.

The next very interesting event was that my employer, with the stud groom as my boss, wanted me to learn how to drive. They had an ancient 2-ton Guy lorry and it was used for carrying fodder to the horses in the field. So they decided to teach me to drive, although I could not go on the road because I was still under age. There was no ignition with this vehicle, the only way to get the engine going was by cranking it. And what a brute it was. I had to be shown exactly how to hold the cranking handle so I would not break my thumb when it backfired, which it did on a regular basis. I learned to drive the lorry and although I never did hit anything I think I gave gateposts a fright when I approached.

I also became skilled at harnessing the large Shire horse and driving it in the cart. Great fun and more learning. The stud groom and the other men were obviously having some amusement at all this, because the next thing they pulled out was a shotgun, to teach me how to shoot. I did not do at all well with a shotgun and it was eventually decided I had no eye for a gun. Besides, I did not particularly like it and eventually began to detest all firearms in general. I still do.

I had started to become very disillusioned with my bicycle and decided an engine would be more appropriate but I certainly did not have the money to invest in one. My parents put their heads together and decided to give me my 21st birthday present in advance.

My father hunted around and produced a pre-war New Imperial motorbike with a 125cc engine, registration number BDN 764. It cost the awful sum of £25. How I came to love that bike and the instant freedom it gave me. No more pedalling and sweating with the wind against me.

I went in for the motorbike test and passed straight away because I have always had some kind of affinity with anything mechanical. Then I wanted to pass my car test and applied for it. This turned out to be another of my fiascos because I failed. Driving a heavy lorry across fields is not the ideal learning for taking a car through city streets. So with my little bit of money I scraped and saved to have proper driving lessons at a school and at the next attempt I passed, in 1947 when I was 17 years of age.

One-day when father was working all day Mother climbed up on the pillion seat and I drove up to see her family at

Wath. We bowled along the Great North Road and I was full of confidence. We made first-class time and the family were astounded at our arrival. We did not have long there but it was all great fun and Mother was in her element. We came back loaded with food goodies and just made it before father returned from his shift duty.

We had all the foods laid out on the table in the family room – a chicken, eggs and vegetables.

"Been a run out?" father queried with interest.

Mother beamed at him. "Yes," she said casually. "We slipped up home for an hour!"

"You what?" and father turned to me. "You must have done some moving. That bike only has a little engine and there were two of you up! I hope you have not blown it!" he said sternly.

Of course I hadn't, but he had to satisfy himself by taking the bike for a very short spin. I was conscious I had hammered that little engine with our joint weights to get us back in time. They built motorbikes tough in 1939 and it was perfectly all right.

Winter came and the stables were filled with horses for the owners and their guests to ride. There were two who stood out. Little Jeff who was the most comfortable horse I have ever ridden with a lovely temperament. I was very jealous of the people who could own such a splendid creature. The other was Captain who was the worst tempered brute of an animal I ever met. He would bite, kick and try and crush the groom against the stable wall. I detested him and he could not stand me – or any other human being either. His redeeming feature was he was a brilliant jumper and also had speed. I had my first hunt on him and discovered he had a mouth like concrete, just about impossible to control, so I let him have his head and muttered a few prayers for myself. He is the only horse I ever encountered that I hated – and I'm certain it was fully reciprocated!

At the end of two years with this job I began to get itchy feet again. There were more rows at home over trivialities. All of a sudden I had had enough of everything, packed a rucksack and walked out. I hitchhiked to London and booked myself into the YWCA. I had very little money so hitchhiked again down to the docks where a liner called the *Dominion Monarch* was moored. It was due to sail to Australia. I stood there on the quayside trying to figure out how to get aboard and stow away but this was quite impossible as there was a man on duty at every gangway.

I suppose I stood out like a sore thumb with wistful longing on my face and unknown to me a dock worker had been watching me. He took my arm and escorted me to his very humble little home where his wife made me a very welcoming cup of tea with a couple of biscuits, which I wolfed down. He talked to me gently and told me to forget about trying to stow away. The security was tight even in those days. I thanked them both so profusely and have never forgotten this kindness to a very young and lonely teenager.

With a heavy heart I walked back many miles to the YWCA and pondered what to do next. Quite by chance, looking at an old newspaper, I saw there was a horse show and gymkhana being held on the outskirts of London. With nothing to lose and virtually out of money I hitched there and walked around all the competitors, eyeing everyone very carefully. One was obviously a show jumping family and I knew nothing about this part of equestrianism. I had my mother's boldness so walked up to the man of the family and told him I was looking for work in the summer. I then proceeded to sell my talents which by now with horses were quite considerable.

He was a very nice man certainly much more pleasant than his wife and rather arrogant daughter and son. He was a dairy farmer and the show jumpers were his son's hobby. Obviously this was a rather affluent family but the wage he offered was poverty stricken as seems to happen everywhere in the horse world.

He offered me a post immediately, to live in and I accepted without hesitation. I had no alternative so I went to Essex near to Saffron Walden.

I was in full charge of the son's show jumping ponies, his sister did not ride and every week end they went to one show or another all around that part of the country. It was hard work doing everything myself but I thrived again and let my parents know where I was, so peace was made. Once again although living in I was treated very much as the 'hired hand' which I resented but I had enough sense to bottle up this feeling. I decided to go through the summer with them then keep my eyes and ears open in the various papers that advertise horsey jobs.

One weekend the toffee nosed son was entered for classes at White city so we all went up there. They stayed in a hotel of course. I was told to kip down in the stables with the horses. No hotel room for me. No washing or toilet facilities and no food. It was this treatment that hardened my heart with a vengeance.

I spotted what I thought was a good job in Warwickshire near Stratford upon Avon. Without even being interviewed I resigned from the current position and hitch hiked – as usual hard up – back to Leicester then took the motorbike and went for an interview. It was a small private yard of just three horses and I would be in total control at all times. The two ladies also wanted someone with a clean driving licence so this job became mine. I said I would start right away which I did after I had checked the living accommodation. This was to be at a farm half a mile away and I examined it very carefully. The farmer's wife, Mrs Bond, was a red cheeked, bosomy woman and I was quite blunt.

"Do you feed people well?" I asked her. "I have had bad experiences in the past," I explained to soften the question a little.

She laughed. "If I didn't, I'd be divorced!"

They became the best and happiest digs of my life. The whole of this family were big readers so I joined the local library too at Stratford. The nearest judo club was at Coventry and I couldn't afford the petrol to go all the way. So I would take the motorbike to Leamington spa and then catch the bus twice a week. I burned the candle at both physical ends and was incredibly hard and fit.

I enjoyed my job. I was in sole charge of three expensive horses and they were kept to the standard I had learned when with Miss Stops. The owners did a certain amount of buying and selling when prospective purchasers would come to examine the horses in the yard. I was always highly complimented at the yard's high standard and I did quite well on tips which were vital revenue. Once a month I would bike home to Leicester to see my parents and, as always, to see Ann again. By now she was a nurse, so there would be frantic rearranging of her shifts. On the odd occasions when she could not do this, we would make up for it on the next visit. Our friendship was very solid, as it is to this day and will be until one of us falls off the twig.

I was very happy indeed but also very conscious I was forever a short of money. It very slowly dawned upon me that the only place to get a decent salary was in a town. I applied to join the Metropolitan police. All through these early days of my life I have landed in fiascos and this was another one. I went up to London for an overnight weekend and numerous interviews and was promptly turned down which shook me. Of course the interviewing policemen sussed me out straight away.

I was a pure country hick with straw in my mouth, totally unsuitable to be trained as a Metropolitan policewoman. I realized then the fact I had left school at 14 did not stand me in great stead. Although well read I was pretty ignorant about life in general. I was very put out about this and my pride collapsed. I put a lot of thought into my position and decided that when spring came I would stretch my wings and do some travelling. This was well before today's 'gap year' had been invented.

I finished with that job when spring came and went back to Leicester and said I wanted to go around Europe. As the age of majority was still 21 years my parents had to agree to sign the passport form but there was no problem there. I think Mother was resigned to the fact I was always going to do what she considered unusual and highly questionable. All father want to know was whether I could handle a knife and he produced a pretty wicked looking sheath knife. I assured him I did know how to handle one because the various boys at the judo club, had taught me knife fighting. He had already worked it out that his daughter was capable and not to be messed with by any one.

So off I went, compete with the precious passport and exactly £5 worth of money in currencies I thought I would need. My dress was thick-ish trousers, riding jacket, a scarf and a rough shirt and hobnailed boots. It was not the most elegant way to dress but very utilitarian. I carried a rucksack filled with cans of food and a small American army mess dish which also doubled as a frying pan. I wore the knife attached to a belt around my waist where it was hidden under the jacket but could be reached in a quick grab.

I hitch hiked down to Dover then crossed over to Calais on the ferry. I set out to walk heading roughly north, eyes everywhere, ears pricked at the foreign language. What little French I had learned at school had completely evaporated. I hadn't gone far when a car pulled up, driven by a woman, inside of which were two Englishmen. They offered me a lift and drove to a small, ramshackle place in the countryside. I was a bit suspicious of all this but said and did nothing. They all piled out of the car went into a disgustingly dirty, broken-down house, then vanished into another room. I stayed in the kitchen and hastily prepared myself a meal with one of my tins of food, then wandered outside to find somewhere to sleep. There was a small barn with plenty of hay and straw, so I threw my sleeping bag down and crept in, quite exhausted with all these strange experiences.

I had not been there any time at all when one of the Englishmen came out, trousers half-undone, and it was obvious what he had in mind. I was out of my sleeping bag in a flash, knife in hand, and jabbed at his belly. He had the shock of his life and retreated so fast he fell over and landed on his seat. I gestured with the knife again and snarled. He received the message and backpedalled, completely falling over in the process. I laughed in his face and gestured with the knife again and that sorted him out. Of course I had precious little sleep that night. In the morning, as soon as it was daylight, I was off again, tramping north, heading towards Belgium.

People were very generous with their lifts and it was amazing the conversations I was able to hold with gestures and limited words. I arrived in Brussels and went straight to the International youth hostel, which was very good indeed. It was Spartan but clean, with bunk beds in rooms for either sex, complete with straw paillasses. There was a kitchen with basic equipment, all clean, so it was easy to rustle up a little meal from my precious store. I made friends with other hitchhikers there and really began to enjoy the experience.

I stayed there two nights and explored the whole of that capital city. I was quite alone but I have never quarrelled with my own company so was perfectly happy and content.

From there I headed north into the Netherlands and once again I found the drivers of various vehicles willing to give me lifts, obviously intrigued by a girl travelling alone.

After exploring Amsterdam, again staying at an international youth hostel, I decided to cross over the Zuider Zee into Friesland. I travelled through the areas where the bulbs were growing and the colours were so riotous they almost hurt my eyes. There was so much to see and take in. I was fascinated with the dam and road over the Zuider Zee but once on the other side, I started I have a quick think. My food stocks were not going to last long at this rate. I could do with staying somewhere and being fed. Taking a chance, I walked up a long path to a farmhouse and with gestures asked if I could spend a couple of nights sleeping on their haystack and do work in exchange for meals. It took an awfully long time for understanding to be reached but I had my way and was shown an appropriate haystack.

The next day I began to earn my keep by doing very extensive housework, which included taking up carpets, putting them on a line and beating them. I scrubbed and polished and took my meals with a gigantic family, which seemed to produce a child per year. They were astounded with me and the head of the family was obviously also intrigued. He reminded me of stories I'd read about South Africa and the Boers. He was large, grizzled and rather taciturn. Before any meal started there was a long reading from the Bible and I was so hungry I couldn't help my stomach rumbling. I nearly curled up with embarrassment then glanced at the man and noted the twinkle in his eyes. He understood and cut it all short.

I spent a few days there and one of the older girls took me out on a bicycle in the evenings, which was another education. There were dikes everywhere – I had never seen so many – all filled with noisy, croaking frogs. The only thing I did not like about this stay was the black bread they served; otherwise the food was very good indeed.

I was given a grand send-off by the whole family as I started tramping along the road, waiting for another lift. I must have travelled a few miles when a car dropped me off near a small bungalow. I felt dreadful and was promptly sick. I went to the door, knocked and was lucky enough to have English-speaking ladies face me. I explained again about sleeping somewhere outside but I was obviously so ill they took me in, bless them. It took a day to throw off this sickness and the ladies' general consensus of opinion was that the problem was caused by the black bread. I have never eaten it since and never will.

The next youth hostel was not far from Arnhem, where the great battle took place. I checked in there then set out to walk the few miles to the cemetery, which held so many of our dead from that of abortive paratroop drop. Walking miles meant nothing to me then because I was so fit and strong. I was enormously impressed by the beautiful way this cemetery was kept but it was sad to see the young ages of so many of the fallen soldiers.

One of my most interesting lifts was with a commercial traveller who had, like so many Dutch people, the most beautiful English. I sat with him all day while he made his various calls, then he invited me to stay the night at his home. I was incredibly lucky with the people who did this and I had a splendid night with his family. When I ate meals with families like this, I always made sure I was the last person to start eating, so that I could see if they had any unusual customs. This family did. They did not eat bread and butter with the fingers like us but cut it with a knife and fork and ate it that way. By using this tactic I saved myself lots of embarrassment.

I left them the next morning and headed towards Luxembourg. My intention had been to go through Germany and then on to Denmark but everyone with whom I had conversed had advised me against going into Germany. It was just too soon after the war and I took notice of what these people said; after all, they had been occupied by the Germans and knew all about them. So I headed south.

There was an excellent international youth hostel at Luxembourg and I still had a little food left in cans, though I was nearly out of money and still had to get back to my own country. I went over the Ardennes where the scenery became so different after the flatness I had recently experienced. Luxembourg was like a little toy country but beautifully kept and clean.

My tough young legs allowed me to hike around everywhere, missing absolutely nothing, but I began to become conscious of the time I had been away from a home and my, by now, very limited financial resources.

I set out for Paris for the first time, going westwards. Lifts were not easy to pick up because it was a public holiday but eventually a large lorry came groaning up a hill and obligingly stopped. Apart from the driver there were three other men in a very large cab and they beckoned me up. I hesitated only long enough to open my jacket buttons and show I was carrying a knife. They were rough men without a word of English between them but they were also nature's gentlemen. They were splendid company but it was late at night before that rather slow-moving lorry entered the outskirts of Paris.

The driver stopped, stepped down from his cab and called to a gendarme. There was a burst of conversation and the French policeman eyed me carefully then beckoned me to step forward. There was nothing else I could do but obey. More than a little scared but wearing a very false brave face, I walked with him and entered a nearby police station.

I was marched up to a desk, behind which stood a very stern-looking policeman, who demanded my passport. I had no French and he had no English but the word passport doesn't need translating. It was quite obvious neither he nor any of the others were going to tolerate a young girl walking around their streets at this godforsaken hour of the night. They were, of course, quite correct.

I gave a shrug and unwrapped my sleeping bag, which was only a blanket sewn up on one side, put my rucksack down as a pillow, had a cup of French coffee, which I thought was superb, then settled down to try and sleep.

I did not have a lot of this because they were a noisy crowd and at midnight they all shook hands with each other or wished each other good-day! This amused me no end. I managed to cat-nap, off and on, then with the dawn I was up and asked for the return of my passport. I think they were going to question me about where I intended to sleep the next night but one of the policemen, with a barrage of French, sorted out some problem and beckoned me.

Rather warily I followed him. We walked, then took a bus, then walked again, to reach a certain building with umpteen stairs to climb to his little flat. There I met his wife and two little girls and I was again invited to spend two nights. I really was incredibly lucky. This formed the start of a gentle friendship between this family and mine. For a small handful of years, visits were exchanged between the two countries but then, as so often happens, we gradually lost touch with each other.

During those two days, Edouard the policeman took me out and about Paris and I saw much which I would never have found alone.

Then it was time to head towards Leicester. He saw me safely settled in a lorry that was going to Calais. The miles sped past and I was content with what I had done, where I had been and what I had seen. I had enough money for a ferry crossing to Dover, then it was hitchhiking from there to Leicester. I was dropped near South Knighton Road, walked down to number 39 and at three o'clock in the morning threw some pebbles against my parents' bedroom window. In no time my father's head appeared. He beamed when he saw me and lights went on everywhere. The door was opened and Mother was already at the gas cooker preparing egg and bacon for me.

How we talked and talked and talked even some more! There was so much to say and to explain. They were avid listeners and I think quite proud of me, although I had done nothing special. Students on gap years now travel much farther but I guess I was a pathfinder for them.

One thing I had decided, although I didn't say just then, was that my days of working with horses were over. I was tired of being constantly poor and although I had no idea what I was going to do, I had decided to go back to my roots – and London.

Chapter VIII

To start with I found London very strange indeed after the isolation of living in the countryside for so many years and being so much alone. It took quite a few days for me to become used to all the traffic, although it was nowhere near as heavy as it is today. And the people! They were everywhere and always so noisy, which confused me more than a little. What on earth did they have to say to each other and in such loud voices all the time? The buses and tube trains were always jam-packed and getting a seat was quite out of the question. As I moved around for the first two or three days I saw how different the dress was to that of country people. I felt that I stuck out like the proverbial sore thumb.

The trouble was, I was in my usual impecunious state and only had my country dress. Because I was so hard up it was once again vital that I get a job with cash on Fridays. Any job as long as the weekly money was there, because I had to pay my board and lodgings on time.

My parents, especially my mother, thoroughly approved of this latest move. By pulling a few strings with old acquaintances they managed to get me into a girls' hostel run by the London Council on the King's Cross Road. It was very good too and I spent quite a bit of time there.

There were three floors, each of which had a dinky little cubicle for one female. There was a single bed, quite comfortable and spotlessly clean, a tiny chest of drawers and the small corner with a curtain to double as a wardrobe. Downstairs there was a large dining room and next to it a big sitting room with comfortable chairs and settees.

Each floor had a bathroom and we had to take turns to reserve this for use and downstairs was a good washroom. My board was £2.10.00 per week (in old money) and Monday to Friday this included breakfast and an evening meal. On the weekends there was also a lunch. The food was not the Savoy standard; very basic but well cooked.

I had never lived with so many people around me and I felt like a complete yokel. Some of the residents were middle-aged and what they were doing there I never did work out. The bulk of the girls were students, bristling with high educational qualifications, which gave them entry to even more detailed courses.

My conversation to start with was very limited indeed because there was so much that I simply did not know. The rest of the girls seemed tremendously sophisticated to me so I was very careful what I said, and when and to whom. But they were all quite friendly and when I discovered that my ignorant status about city life did not disturb them at all, I gradually began to make a few friends.

It was critical that I obtained work as soon as possible and I managed to get a job with the Kerbside Kar Kleaners, about a quarter of a mile away towards the city. We were all issued with lumbering bicycles which had a big plate emblazoned with the firm's name plus a bucket, chamois leather, sponges and car polish. The business consisted solely of cleaning people's cars parked at the side of a road or in a car park while owners were at work.

We could be sent on our cycles just about anywhere in the capital and this was how I came to know London. The pay was not very good but it could be bolstered with tips. The few men employed by the firm made sure they always got the car cleaning jobs at the hospitals, where the consultants always left a generous tip. After I had been there a few weeks I found this out and objected strenuously. I considered there should be a system where the tips were shared out at the end of each day. It goes without saying this did not make me very popular. Once again, I started to look around elsewhere.

There was a job advertised for a switchboard operator at Remington Rand in Oxford Street. I applied and was taken on but on that very first day I realized I was pretty much out of my depth. Working a solitary switchboard was all very well but being one of a battery of girls, sitting in a row before complicated boards, was rather more difficult.

The money was better so I tried and tried, but in those days all business had to be routed through switchboards and each girl had to work very fast indeed. I tried my best but became increasingly worried. Then one day the supervisor took me to one side. She explained that I was simply not good enough but that she had heard of a firm of solicitors off Park Lane who had a small board and wanted an operator and receptionist. I took the hint and applied. To my surprise the job was mine and I spent many happy months working for these solicitors.

Mother was absolutely delighted that at long last I was doing a 'proper' job and that I had turned my back on horses. Not quite though, because one of the solicitors kept a horse at livery and used to ride it on Rotten Row for exercise for himself as well as the horse. He learned about my background and asked if I would like to ride his horse for him when court cases stopped him from doing this. I jumped at the chance and made a point of keeping some trousers and appropriate shoes at work.

I and many of the girls at the hostel wished to take complete advantage of our time in London but we were all in the same boat financially. Very short of money. We soon got around this problem by going in a small group to the theatre or a show of choice and queuing for the very cheap seats in the gods. We would take it in turns over many hours and by this tactic I and the others were able to see and enjoy every show in London. I often sat in the gods looking over the rail at the people down below in the best seats, wondering about them. Since then I have been to shows in the best seats and locked up at the eager, young faces in the gods. I know exactly what they are thinking and feeling.

On Sundays, if my few friends were otherwise engaged, I would take myself off out and walk and walk and walk. That is the very best way to see a city and I really began to know my London. I even crossed the river and explored around the Elephant and Castle.

I had joined the Budokwai judo club, which was *the* club, so I had friends there and would attend at least twice a week for practice. In 1951 the Festival of Britain was held in London and the club were asked to give a number of judo demonstrations. I was very surprised and more than a little flattered to be invited. It was the first time I had been before an audience but luckily I had no nerves and quite enjoyed the experience. My horizons had expanded with a vengeance but I had not forgotten my vow to go to Australia when I was 'of age' (21 years old).

In the meantime, I qualified for a week's holiday and went up to Yorkshire with the sole intention of asking Bob to get me down the pit. I don't know what strings he pulled, he was an overman by now, but down the pit I went. Going in the cage for the first time with its drop at speed was a little nerve wracking but I made myself stand still with bent knees to compensate for the reduction in speed when we reached the appropriate level.

I was taken to see the pit ponies first and how well-kept they were too. Before going down Bob had checked that I had neither lighter nor matches with me, but I knew better than to jeopardize our lives in a pit which held gas.

It was the most remarkable experience and I take my hat off to men who go underground to hew for coal. We had a lot of walking to do – and not walking along a pavement either. I was dressed in rough clothes, wore kneepads, had a safety helmet on and from this ran the power to operate my headlamp.

Nobody knows what real black is like until they've been down a coal mine and doused all the lights. It's weird to the point of being terrifying.

Bob took me into seams so low we had to crawl on hands and feet and here the kneepads came into their own. Then he took me up a seam, held his gas detection lamp up and very gradually the flame began to change colour, warning there was gas.

The next experience was with a group of miners when I was invited to drill my own shot hole. I wondered why they grinned at me as they placed a leather pad over my shoulder. The drill was then lifted up onto this pad; it was not unlike a pneumatic drill used to dig up roads. When they started it up, I swear that all my teeth left my gums, the vibration was colossal. But I stuck it out. I was not going to cry chicken before these men.

The next interesting activity came from the shot firer, who placed sticks of explosive down the holes, then nodded to Bob. He led us right away from the area, leaving the shot firer to remove the dangerous detonators from a locked pouch attached to his belt. After a while he came back to us, holding a square black box with two handles. He received the nod from Bob, connected two wires to his box, rested his hands on the handle, received another nod from Bob and down went the plunger.

We were all leaning against the coal wall, which gave a savage jolt. At the same time an acrid stench of explosives started to come back to us from the ventilation. We continued to sit then Bob gave a nod and the shot firer went back alone to check that all the explosives had gone off and there wasn't one hanging around waiting to bang just as men approached to shovel coal.

It was a unique experience for me and I knew I was privileged to be part of such activity. I guess there are not many girls around who have drilled their own hole underground and been present when detonators and explosives were used. This whole day made such a vivid impression on me that even now, many, many decades later, I can relive every moment underground with the Yorkshire colliers.

We headed back towards the shaft at a faster pace because Bob nipped two wires above the belt which carried the coal, stopped it and we jumped on, but I was warned to keep very flat and not lift my head under any circumstances, because the belt went through some narrow places.

After this, we went in the cage again and he took me down to the very bottom of the shaft. Here were installed the great pumps to keep the pit as dry as possible, because overhead ran a river. It was also at this point, decades before, that there had been a huge explosion from gas. A whole shift of men and boys were underground and they all died instantly. All that could be done was to seal off the entrance and it was kept like that for quite a few years before the geologists decided the fire had burned itself out and it was safe to open up again.

The finale was going to the pithead baths – and how we needed them! Bob sent a runner on ahead to warn everybody a female was coming in and there was a panicky mass evacuation. How I revelled in getting clean and it made me appreciate how the men enjoyed the pithead baths instead of having to go home, covered in muck, to get clean there.

I did not have a lot to say to Grandma or anyone else. I was still in a daze after such incredible experiences and filled with sheer admiration for all the men who worked in such a place under such dangerous conditions.

I did not really recover my equilibrium until I was back again in the Mary Curzon hostel at London. After some experiences it can take quite a time to settle down once more.

The next big event was my 21st birthday when I became an adult officially, answerable to no one but myself. I went straight round to Australia House and applied to go on their immigration scheme, which cost just £10 provided the migrant stayed for a minimum of two years. At this particular time they were mainly interested in getting families to migrate, so I was told I would have to wait but that my turn would come eventually.

I had read a lot about the country. *We of the Never Never* by Mrs Aeneus Gunn. *Robbery Under Arms* by Rolf Boldrewood and though I am not particularly fond of poetry (even the variety that rhymes not today's modern stuff which doesn't) but I liked the poems *Clancy Of The Overflow* and *The Man From Snowy River* by Banjo Patterson as well as *Waltzing Matilda* by him. I was well read on other countries but I had worked it out that I would see more on a voyage to Australia and that was really the object of the exercise. I could not get enough of exploring strange places. Someday I would have to settle down, like everyone else had to eventually, but that time had not yet arrived.

I sailed from Southampton on the SS *New Australia* on the exact day the King died in 1952 and our monarch became a Queen. The union flag was at half-mast on the liner. Mother had come to see me off but she was not allowed on the ship.

She called up to me and explained what was going on. I dutifully handed over my passport, registration document and all other paperwork, which was now irrelevant.

Mother did not stay long because it was not far from where my parents had lived when they first married at the house whose name they gave to me. I watched her proudly walk away, holding back her tears in her tough Yorkshire way, then I went and explored below to find my cabin which would be my home for the next month.

My cabin was down on D Deck and held six bunk beds. My travelling companions were all there and it certainly was a squeeze but there was a good atmosphere and even though I was the youngest I did not feel uncomfortable. Two of the women were middle-aged marrieds and their husbands were in cabins with males. I had already heard there were 1,500 of us on this liner, half of whom were children. I also gradually learned, as the days went by, that the Master at Arms had his work cut out keeping law and order and the children under complete control. Rather him than me.

Life on board a liner is like nothing else on earth and has to be experienced to be understood. The routine is so totally different and commenced with lifeboat drill in which we all had to muster at our lifeboat stations wearing Mae Wests. There was considerable confusion and it crossed my mind to wonder what exactly would happen if we had to abandon ship for some reason.

Because there were so many of us, meals had to be held in sittings. I was in the first while the rest of my cabin mates were in the second. I became quite fascinated with this very unusual life and, once we had gone through the Bay of Biscay, I wallowed in the wonderful sunshine.

The first port of call was at Algiers and I was off that liner like a rocket, eager to see everything possible. I walked around everywhere, then began to climb a steep hill without a thought in the world. Youth is so innocent. I was only entering the Kasbah and getting some very strange and most unfriendly looks from the Arab males who were loitering around. Very luckily I spotted my cabin mates, who were doing the same thing but had been able to afford a guide.

They called me over to join them and when the guide realized I had come up there alone he nearly threw a fit. He ushered us into a little group to go back down to the harbour and now the Arab men were very close to our rear. They showed their hostility and their shouts confirmed their aggression. I swung around, ready for a fight if necessary and stayed with the group but walking backwards and facing the men. I don't think I can have looked particularly friendly myself because when they found themselves face-to-face with a belligerent white female they backed off but continued with a barrage of uncomplimentary remarks. It was a good object lesson for me. I was not in Britain now. I was in a strange land with a very different culture where the status of the female was well below that of a prized camel.

When we reached the harbour it was time to embark again and I chipped in the few coins I could afford for the guide. It was rather pathetic but I only had five pounds to last me for the whole of the four-week voyage. My usual impecunious state.

There was plenty to do on the liner, with umpteen classes on every subject under the sun as well as entertainment. There was a very small swimming pool and for those who just wished to relax, plenty of deckchairs. I soon discovered a small high deck called the Poop Deck and I got into the habit of spending many hours there, basking in the sun, looking around and wondering about life in general.

My intention was to spend my two years in Australia then go on to Tokyo to join the Kodokan, the most famous judo club in the world. I planned to try and get work of any kind, even domestic, at our embassy. The best laid plans of mice and men do indeed go awry and fate had other ideas for me but as we headed down to the Suez Canal I was still in blissful ignorance.

We reached Port Said early on 14th February, Valentine's Day. To me it was just another day and after breakfast I climbed high to my favourite seat. We sailed before noon as we had not been allowed ashore, owing to the political situation and the short time in harbour. Our liner had to be available to sail down the canal in a convoy because it is not particularly wide.

A number of chairs on the poop deck were occupied by girls who had to go to a second sitting lunch. They asked me to keep my eye on them because it was amazing how deckchairs could vanish when left alone.

I was sitting in one, gazing to both sides of the canal as we slowly sailed through, when quite suddenly a man appeared from somewhere and promptly sat down in the chair next to me. I hastened to warn him that they were reserved but he made it clear that he had not the slightest intention of moving. Instead he was going to chat to me.

And that is exactly how I met Roy Peel, my future husband. He had such lovely eyes and was rather handsome, to put it mildly. To my utter astonishment I felt an instant attraction. I had known plenty of boys before in various judo clubs but none had ever turned me on like this. Was I going mad? It was as if the rest of the world, the crowded liner and life in general had ceased to exist. I felt suddenly that I was alone in a special dimension and yet not alone with this man. I could see he was a bit older than me but I felt very comfortable with him. I knew nothing about him but all of a sudden I knew everything there was to know. It was all very weird.

He grinned at me, I chuckled back and it was obvious we were both content in each other's company. The sky was the most brilliant of blues, which made such a harsh contrast with the colour of the sand. The girls came back from lunch for their deckchairs, assessed the situation and tactfully removed their chairs to go elsewhere.

Then it was time to retire for our evening meal. All he did was lift an eyebrow in a silent question and I replied with an equally quiet nod.

He was travelling with two of his mates and they were all in one cabin on C deck, so at every port of call the three boys went off together and I followed my usual practice of wandering alone. After that, of course, the two of us spent all our time together, talking gently and learning about each other – although there wasn't one kiss in sight.

The weather became extremely hot in the Red Sea and as we passed the country of Saudi Arabia it never entered either of our heads that one day we would become familiar with this country. So strange does life become. We then had the fairly long haul across the Indian Ocean to Ceylon now called Sri Lanka, home of the aggressive Tamil Tigers.

Once again I explored by myself but this time I was more prudent, after the Algiers' experience. I kept to the main roads and if I decided to visit any shops I made sure there were other people around who looked civilised. But I was only able to buy a few postcards because of my poverty. After sailing again I met Roy once more on the poop deck and experienced something else very unusual.

Night falls rapidly in the tropics and the sky was inky black. It was so hot, almost difficult to breathe. Then we were treated to an enormous display of nature's power. We watched, quite spellbound, as a mighty electrical storm lit up the sky, but without thunder. It was silent and mesmerizing as the sky repeatedly flashed with vivid forks of lightning so powerful they lit up the ocean, which did not have even the smallest ripple on its surface. Our ship, underneath all this, seemed very puny and insignificant.

The next port of call was Freemantle for Perth and again I was one the first off on one of my explorations. I went right up into Perth and walked around everywhere until even my tough legs started to complain. I adored Perth, indeed I have never heard anyone have a bad word for this city in the State of Western Australia.

A few more days across the Australian Bight and we neared Melbourne. A whole month had gone by and now our arrival was imminent. It was a case of packing everything, filling in reams of paperwork and saying goodbye to everyone I had met during the last month. Except Roy. I knew we would meet again. We both knew it was inevitable.

Me, aged 18 months, with my mother, 1931.

Aged three.

Bo and Me (aged six years).

Aged 17 years on Little Jeff ~ the most comfortable horse I have ever ridden.

Aged 19 years on valued two-wheeled motorised transport.

Aged 20 years.

Aged 19 years, hitchhiking around Europe.

Aged 19 years, at home with my beloved books.

Our wedding day.

Getting to know a non poisonous constrictor at Brisbane wildlife centre, 1954.

Roy and I on horseback in the Australian bush, 1954.

Riding back in the UK, sometime in the 1960s.

Roy with Tau, our first Siamese cat.

Me and Tau, at home ~ 1970s.

On a visit to a tropical flower house in the Channel Islands, 1980s.

Me in our flat with Tai, our Havana and Sadiq, a chocolate point Siamese.

Me, aged 62, with Tai and Katy (a Devon Rex).

My last ride, aged 72 years.

Roy and I on our last day out together.

Rory and I on a river cruise from Gloucester, 2002.

Aged 79 years.

My latest motorised transport (8mph!).

Chapter IX

The married families disembarked first and all we single people waited until last. We went by a ramshackle coach to a hostel reception centre, my inquisitive eyes looking everywhere as usual. I was given a little bunk bed in a kind of shed and never saw Roy for the rest of that day.

The Australians had done all this before. They had a list of various types of accommodation and one was for a single girl. I asked for that and so found myself in Drummond Street in a funny little old house. There were other people lodging there each with their own miniscule room. Mine was very tiny indeed, just room for a bed and tiny cupboard. There was a communal kitchen and bathroom and as I eyed everyone up, girls as well as boys, I decided that some were definitely questionable and to be on my guard.

It was a holiday weekend and as soon as it ended I knew I had to find work. In the meantime I went back to the hostel and picked up the threads with Roy. He and his two mates were on the verge of moving out to Middle Brighton, where the three of them would share an enormous room. We exchanged addresses but there was nothing else we could do.

I quickly found work for myself as a clerk, shuffling bits of paper around again, but it paid a reasonable wage, which was my priority. Roy and his two mates also found work, with an insurance company, although the three of us knew this was but temporary until they found their feet.

It was winter there and cold. Wind blasted out from the Antarctic and it rained every bit as much as in Manchester. Roy and I met twice a week as we continued our gentle courtship. After about three months the three boys decided to go into the bush to work for an organization which was drilling for coal – brown coal not black. They would work as offsiders to the skilled men who operated the drilling rigs. It was in New South Wales, right out in the bush.

As soon as Roy had gone, my time in Melbourne went flat. I missed his Yorkshire humour and good companionship so I decided I would move on and go to Brisbane in the State of Queensland, where there was a good judo club. As always, I decided to hitch-hike to save money. My heavy goods had travelled in tin trunk kept in the ship's hold. I paid for and arranged for it to go to Brisbane to be collected in the near future and I also paid two Australian shillings for insurance.

Then I was off again and immediately got a lift in the car of a bush couple who took me right to Aldbury, near the state boundary. They were cattle ranchers with a large station in the bush and I found them fascinating to talk to. Although third-generation Australians, they still referred to Britain as 'home', which I found very touching.

In the little bush town of Aldbury I had a quick wash at a department store and was on the road again. I had walked no distance when a huge car stopped and asked where I was going. I explained I was heading towards Sydney and was told to hop in the vacant seat in the front. In the rear seats were a man and an oldish lady. The car was a powerful 25hp Wolsely and built on the lines of a tank. The driver was a thick-set man about 40 and the second I slammed the door the car took off as if it had produced wings.

Seatbelts had not yet been invented and I noted that his idea of driving was foot on the boards. At the same time he kept popping some kind of tablet into his mouth and also taking a drink from a bottle. I became quite frightened and I don't scare easily. In the middle of the night I flashed a look at the male passenger behind me and he gave a peculiar nod so I reached over and removed the ignition key.

I thought the driver would then have a fit of fury and he told me if I felt like that I could get out. It was at some godforsaken hour of the night, in the pitch dark and all I knew was we had passed through Gudagai, where the dog sat on his tucker box, and starved to death as he waited for a master who never returned.

I was beaten and knew it so handed the key back and resigned myself to whatever was going to happen. Obviously the man in the rear had no authority whatsoever. Then eventually the car had to slow down because we came across floodwater. As the vehicle halted men appeared and engaged the driver in conversation. I couldn't hear a word that was said so took the chance to speak to the other man.

"What's going on?" I hissed with worry.

The man nodded at the woman and turned so she couldn't hear. "We're taking her to a mental institution and she is his Mother. He's taking benzedrine tablets and that's whisky his drinking."

I was absolutely horrified. "Can't you take over?" I asked with agitation.

He shook his head firmly. "He might get violent. I've enough on keeping her quiet!"

I simply did not know what to do for the best. This was a situation right out of Jane Eyre by Charlotte Brontë. Then activity started and us three had to get out of the car, scramble into a huge lorry while the car itself would be towed with the driver at the wheel. It was a real performance handling the woman and the man certainly had his hands full coping with her. I understood his invidious position although mine was not much better but I decided to stay where I was on the principle of "better the devil you know".

Eventually we were through the floodwaters and I even managed to fall asleep from exhaustion and mental stress. The car stopped at Sydney's famous bridge where I stumbled out. The driver offered to take me on further but no way. I exchanged a sympathetic look with the mental attendant and wished him well. I then picked up lifts in slow, old-fashioned lorries and eventually reached West Wallsend, a tiny bush town where I saw hitching rails were available everywhere for when the stock riders came to town.

Roy was not far away and I managed to get a message sent to him. He had the shock of his life when he turned up and promptly booked me into a hotel because I was just about asleep standing up. He did not approve of this form of travel and persuaded me that the rest of the journey to Brisbane should be in a civilized airplane.

I counted my money very carefully and decided I might as well go for broke, so I ended up in Brisbane, again fairly late at night. I had the telephone number of the top Judoka and rang him and explained my predicament. As good as gold he turned up, booked me into a hotel for the night and the next morning arranged for me to have lodgings with a single female much older than myself.

Jobs were thin on the ground. In those days, so many decades ago, the economy of the country was decided by the quality and quantity of the wool clip. That year it had failed. I obtained a job with a small mail order firm and decided to be independent with my living. At the same time my trunk was delivered and had been broken into. I was heartbroken. Treasures from home had all gone. I told the police but nothing was ever done to my knowledge. I certainly never heard anything else or received anything back. My foresight with the insurance was a little compensation but I would rather have had my property back.

I moved into a quite large hostel on the banks of the Brisbane River. It was a mixed hostel but there were no problems because the sexes slept on different landings. I saw the top judo man, a doctor who had a small place in the bush as well and he took me out there with him. When he realized my equestrian knowledge he took me riding in the bush and promptly gave me a horse! To say that I was taken aback is a total understatement. It was a gelding, a retired racehorse, and surplus to his requirements because, unbeknown to me, he had decided to sell the property.

I had the horse shod then rode him back to the hostel, which included using a ferry. The horse was not very thrilled by this experience. I had noted a large field nearby with many horses in it, so I turned him loose. Two days later, when I went to catch him, there wasn't a horse in sight. They had all been taken away for sale and because I hadn't the sense to learn his hoof brand I could not identify him at all. That was my solitary experience of owning my own horse! Perhaps it all turned out for the best because I could not have managed to keep him on the money I earned after I had paid my board and lodging.

I did not like the job I was at so moved to another, where, initially, I had to work in a factory on the boring job of folding a piece of cardboard to make a tea packet. Then I muscled my way into the office and the switchboard. The pay was not brilliant so I kept my ears and eyes open and scanned the local newspaper and eventually ended up working for a construction firm. It was the same kind of work but much better money. I stayed there for quite a while. At the same time my parents had decided to take the plunge and come out themselves. I could well imagine my father's timidity over such a giant step but I knew my mother would win on this one. It would give them the chance to see something of the world as well as me.

The next excitement was to learn that Roy had become disillusioned with life in the bush and planned to come up to Brisbane. I had met some other nice young fellows but there wasn't one who turned me on like Roy Peel. I hastily arranged accommodation for him in the hostel and had a shrewd idea it would not be long before his two mates followed.

He came up for Christmas and we went down to Mermaids' Beach for a long weekend. He nearly drowned. We were both good swimmers, quite powerful. For a few pennies we hired a little waterbed to play around at the edge of the surf. I was on the surf bed with Roy swimming alongside. A large wave came along and we were separated. Afterwards I learned what happened. Roy was caught by the undertow and every time he tried to push up and reach the surface he was slammed down again. He said it was a queer sensation, starting to drown. It was quiet and peaceful and it would have been so easy to breathe in lungfuls of water.

Quite suddenly a lifeguard appeared alongside me and with one brawny arm dragged me to the beach then went back and rescued Roy. By the time they had him out, his skin had gone a pasty colour and was goose-pimpled with cold. This seemed ridiculous in the heat but it was lack of oxygen in his body. Roy vowed he would never go into the surf again and he did not. I did a few times but very cautiously.

We took it into our heads to be independent and opened a little grocery shop by pooling our savings. What we did not know, because we lacked the experience, was to check out the area first. A supermarket opened nearby after a few months and we were lucky to sell the shop eventually and get our savings back.

So it was back to office work again. Roy was a good shorthand typist and I could still manage the switchboard, do some clerical work and act as a receptionist.

My parents had arrived and were settled more quickly than us. Roy had started to consider our future when we married. As it happened, we were not to have any children, but we weren't to know that then. He began to talk about us returning to Britain. I was unsure what to do for the best.

We were married on 24th October 1953 and spent a fortnight's honeymoon on Hayman Island in the Great Barrier Reef. We travelled up by flying boat and this was a fantastic fortnight. The hotel had been constructed in the shape of an H and the guests lived in private cabins, beautifully furnished, half a dozen paces from the sea. It was quite idyllic.

It was a let-down to return from Hayman to start this life again. One day at work something very peculiar happened. I had been given an old typewriter and though I wasn't very good I could manage to use it a little. One morning, seemingly of their own accord, my fingers typed "Jim Ryder swore as his kneepad slipped." I stared at these words blankly then pictures filled my mind and I knew I had a short story.

At this time we lived in a dinky little rented flat and by coaxing I was able to obtain the loan of this typewriter to use in the flat. How I worked on writing that short story. My scenes were good as were my characters so when I had finished it I sent it off with hope in my heart.

It came bouncing back saying I had a good story, the magazine liked my 'Pit of Fear' but they could not make me an offer until I had 'cleaned it up'. I hadn't the faintest idea what they meant. Writing is an art which cannot be learned from a book, only from experience. Although I had always been, and still was, a great reader, it was for the story content alone and not the construction.

I was hopelessly confused and there was no one to whom I could turn. Roy said to let it go until we get back to Britain, because this was what we had decided to do. The climate of Queensland, which can be exceedingly humid, did not agree with me at all, so after much thought we decided that instead of moving back to Melbourne, we would add a few more thousand miles and go all the way back to Britain.

We arranged to sail back on an Italian liner. We would disembark in Genoa and cross Europe by train. Roy was a real steam buff and this was his choice. In those days only the rich could afford to fly and aeroplanes took a long time. Besides, there is nothing joyful about sitting in a flying cigar tube for umpteen hours, unable to stretch your legs properly, eating from little trays balanced near one's lap and trying to use toilets which are miniscule. I have done a lot of it since and consider there is nothing pleasurable about flying. It certainly cannot remotely compare to life on a liner. It's true the journey takes longer but if this can be turned into a holiday – it can be fascinating going ashore at the various ports of call.

The liner was the MV *Flotta Laura* and she sailed from Brisbane, no long journey down to Sydney or Melbourne. It was a class boat, in other words first and second-class, which restricted perambulations. The second-class passengers had one portion of the ship for walking while the first class had the other which was the better! We were not at all worried about this. As a married couple we had our own cabin, which was very different indeed from the way in which we travelled out. The only point which bothered me was this was a smaller vessel and I don't have the best of stomachs at sea.

My parents stayed behind to do another year because they too had gone out as migrants, so had to be there two years. They were also exploring and investigating and soaking up the atmosphere, because if they came back, which I suspected they would, it would be back to the humdrum routine of the normal working-class British life.

There were times on that voyage when I was heartily glad it was a class boat because the Italian opera company were returning in first. Even in second we could hear them practicing all the time.

Our route this time was up the eastern coast of Australia and we had to have a pilot as we sailed past the 1,000-mile stretch of the Great Barrier Reef. He would leave us at Thursday Island at the tip of Cape York. We were then due to sale across the Arafura Sea to Indonesia before heading for Singapore. More new places to explore!

We were only two days out of Brisbane when I saw an enormous shark leap from the sea. I shouted to Roy but by that time he turned it had fallen back into the water and he could only gauge its size by its splash. There was no time to identify whether it was a tiger, white or whale shark. Whatever, it was frightening. Nobody swimming in the sea would have a chance against such a brute.

After a few days at sea, the ship's daily newspaper informed us that we would not be calling at Indonesia because of serious political troubles there and that we would sail direct to Singapore instead. A pity to miss a place we would never have the chance to see again, but these things happen. What it did mean, though, was that the ship might be short of fresh water by the time we reached Singapore. We were warned that we may have to bathe or a shower in seawater, not the kindest of substances for the skin and useless for getting a lather with soap.

As usual, we were among the first ashore to explore. The Far East definitely has something quite unique, unlike anything in Europe. After 10 days eating Italian food I craved some lovely English stodgy food, so we went to the famous Little's for lunch and I indulged myself in a lovely suet pudding. At a nearby table was a tea planting set who promptly looked down their noses at us as we were so obviously off the liner. How I dislike people like this. When I was a humble girl groom all those years ago at Great Limber, I was very much at the bottom of the pile of social status. Whenever the Earl of Yarborough rode through the village and saw me he always nodded his head and politely removed his bowler hat. One cannot beat the manners of the aristocracy, they are genuine, possibly reinforced by being potty trained by a Norland nanny. Manners to them are as natural as breathing, while the couple who were looking across at us were nobodies in my estimation because of their artificiality.

We went to the fabulous Tiger Balm Gardens, which was an experience in itself where Roy noted something which had escaped me. He pointed out the very wide and deep storm drains on both sides of the roads. They had not been built for decoration and we decided we would not like to live there when it rained!

As we sailed again, preparations were being made for a "crossing the line" ceremony for those who had never crossed the equator before. We had done this, of course, on the voyage out, but on the SS *New Australia* there were simply too many people for this kind of fun.

Roy was chosen as the King and me as his Queen, which amused us no end, but before we put on our ceremonial robes, bathing costumes went on first, as this hilarious activity was to take place by the ship's swimming pool. Certain good-humoured people had being press-ganged into being the victims and there were chuckles all around as Roy stood up and pronounced sentence on all of them. They were all in bathing suits and had the dubious pleasure of ice going down their necks and eggs being broken over their heads; then they were slung into the pool. As Roy had suspected, as the court ended we followed suit and it was great fun all around with certificates being issued which confirmed that King Neptune had allowed us into his territory.

Then it was off again to Sri Lanka for more exploring at Colombo. We went on a short tour then ended up being driven to the top of Mount Lavinia. There is a hotel right at the very peak, not very large and colonial in construction. Palm trees graced the place, as did brilliantly green grass. It was all so much kinder on the eye after the drabness of Australia with its fawns and browns.

We sat on a seat and had the most stunning view of white sand beaches below us and the blue of the ocean. Now and again a palm tree would drop a coconut and muted sounds from the waves below blended with other soft sounds of tropical birds chit-chatting and insects murmuring, as the delicate breeze rustled grasses together. We sat until night descended and it was time to go. Our liner would soon sail.

As we stood, a kind of fairytale spell was broken forever and we returned to the prosaic world of reality but neither of us ever forgot that dreamy afternoon atop Mount Lavinia.

Our next port of call was Egypt and Roy arranged for us to tour properly. We docked at Suez, where the tour was to commence. Quite a few people had also elected to take the tour and when we landed a large fleet of Cadillacs awaited, each of which would hold six people. While we were away on this tour, the liner would continue to sail up the canal to Port Said, ready for us to re-join it.

We were the first away and headed for Cairo. There was desert on both sides of the road and the sand was not of the Blackpool variety. We reached the capital for morning coffee, which was served by giant Nubians. These people are coal black and very tall, with immense dignity. Roy was 6ft 3 inches tall and most were his height or more.

The very narrow streets were jam-packed with people but after my Algiers experience we kept very close to the guide allocated to us. We went into the great museum, which had a special display of gold and other artefacts from King Tutankhamen's tomb. To our surprise we were invited into the Great Mosque after exchanging our footwear for flip-flops. We were shown a wall of gold for when King Farouk worshipped there. I simply had to reach out my fingers and touch it. It was such a delightful yellow colour and warm with invitation.

From there we went out to the Great Sphinx and I spotted a line of horses and camels. The latter I ignored and slowly strolled down the line of horses, all pure Arabians. I had taught Roy to ride in Australia but he was not very good. He had started too late in life and was rather too tall. I was entranced and our guide saw this.

I picked out a stallion, as I had never ridden one before. The attendant thought he was going to just gently lead me around. I soon dispelled that idea and touched with my heels. The stallion took off like a rocket and I realized instantly why he wore a long curb bit with a tight chain. It was all right by me if he wanted to gallop – and gallop he certainly did. He felt different to any other horse I had ever ridden. He carried his head and tail high with natural arrogance. His steps were so smooth. He appeared to float and me with him. The sand was a brown blur with the horizon a mottled blue vision. I leaned forward, thoroughly enjoying myself and marvelling. I felt powerful and regal on that stallion.

There was a yell from behind me and I was aghast to see Roy coming after me – on a mare that was bravely intent on catching up with her boyfriend. Roy looked precarious in the saddle, lurching very badly. It never entered my head that he would come after me. I presumed he would wait for my return. Not a bit of it.

I pulled up that stallion with some effort. He had burned off his first enthusiasm and, although jiggling a little, he awaited the mare's arrival. When they caught up Roy's face was bright red and he was covered with sweat, so we turned the two horses and walked back, rather sedately. Roy had done incredibly well not to fall off but his legs had gone to jelly with the effort. I had experienced this myself in the past.

It was quite peaceful then to examine the pyramids and the Sphinx, whose nose had been shot off long ago by Napoleon's artillery men. Upon our return to Cairo we were thrust back into the noise, dust and dirt, where yet another tour had been arranged. It was the kind of day when one experience followed another in quick succession. In no time it was dark and we boarded our car for the drive along the canal to Port Said. On the way we passed our liner and the people left aboard waved at us. We waved and yelled back at them from open windows.

At Port Said we were dropped at the docks but here we had an unpleasant experience. There were many Arabs around and, although quiet, they looked threatening. They certainly had no love for Westerners. We passengers from the liner were backed up against the dock gates where the men formed a cordon around the women and stood guard in a stand-off. Our guide became agitated and arranged for the gates to be unlocked to allow us to go inside and stand on the quayside until our liner docked.

The next day's sailing meant we entered a new world. Since leaving Brisbane we had been in constant sunshine but now we hit the weather of Europe. It was November, we were on the home stretch, there were heavy clouds overhead and it turned very cold.

One particular night as we were having our evening meal, for no apparent reason the Italian passengers all jumped up from their seats and, in a mad crowd, rushed out on deck, jabbering like a pack of monkeys. Naturally we Brits had to follow to discover the cause of all this excitement.

As we arrived on deck we were greeted by the most atrocious smell imaginable. It was very dark and whilst our noses quivered our eyes were drawn to one side. Our liner, which had seemed large, was suddenly dwarfed as we sailed past the erupting volcano of Stromboli. The stink of chemicals and acids filled the air while flames belched into the night sky. Only the tiniest plume of smoke appeared to sit just above the flames. Dinner was forgotten as Stromboli treated us to an incredible firework display. We could not tear our eyes from the magnificent spectacle. We knew we would not see the like of it again.

It poured with rain at Naples where quite a few of the Italian passengers disembarked. The holiday atmosphere had vanished; we were nearly back to the nitty-gritty of life. How and where were we going to end up and doing what? The voyage ended at Genoa, where it poured with rain again and we were glad to get to the railway station and enter our pre-booked railway sleeper.

That night we lay in our bunks, muffled against the unaccustomed cold. Sometime during the night I awoke and peered between the curtains. The train had halted at the Frontier Post and I looked into brilliant moonlight. There was a pine covered slope and glistening snow. It was amazing to see snow after nearly four years. We reached the French coast, as I had done all these years ago, and soon we were looking up at the white cliffs of Dover, which had emerged from the mist. I marvelled at all that had happened since I was last here, on the day the Queen became monarch.

It took us ages to get through Customs with six suitcases and a portable radio. How delightfully British it all looked, with a welcoming Bobby wearing his helmet. Then it was another train to London and we prepared to do the rounds of our families, both of which, fortunately, were very small.

No matter where we eventually ended up nor what we did to earn our living, I had determined that I was going to be a writer, although I had enough sense to realize that it would be a mighty task given the fact that I was virtually uneducated, having left school at 14 years of age to suit myself.

Roy knew about my burning ambition and approved but he warned me that it was going to be very tough. That I realized but this only made me all the more determined to succeed no matter how long it might take. We were still young, we were healthy and it is better to have ambition than to loll around in a useless dead-end.

Chapter X

The 1960s opened with the tail-end of erratic activity from the fifties. We dutifully visited our respective and fortunately small families, by whom we were examined, studied, questioned and nearly poked and prodded as if we were cattle for sale at the nearby farmers' stock market. In a way it was understandable because it is only human to be curious but after a while it became more than a little irksome. We put up with it until we decided we had had enough and it was time to move on and get some roots planted.

Before we left Australia we had decided there were areas in which we did not wish to live. Roy did not want to go back to Leeds and I had the same feeling about Leicester. London was quite out of the question because it was too big, too crowded and too noisy. After a detailed study of the map of Britain we both plumped for Bristol and the West Country. It was all new to us yet appeared to be the gateway to magnificent countryside as well as the sea.

So down to Bristol we went and into some temporary digs. Soon afterwards we obtained a mortgage and bought ourselves a 1939 vintage semi-detached house at Little Stoke. We also both obtained employment with what was then the engines division of the B.A.C. but is now known as Rolls Royce. It was clerical work and I knew I would end up being bored stiff.

At the same time my rejected short story 'Pit of Fear' kept nagging at me, so I wrote and rewrote it and sent it out constantly, but it would bounce back, rejected just as fast. I wrote another short story called *His First Day* and sent it to the *Courier* magazine, who promptly accepted it and contacted me with a copy of the magazine plus a cheque for six guineas. I was quite over the moon with pride and delight. This was the first little bit of encouragement I had received. This magazine no longer exists but I have always had a very warm spot in my heart for their name.

It still riled me about 'Pit of Fear' so I did the only sensible thing and filed it away for the future. A few years afterwards I sold the first British rights to *Reveille*, also now vanished, and they paid me very well indeed.

My real ambition was to write a book and fortunately I had enough sense to write about a subject that I knew and understood intimately, namely horses. I remembered back to my girlhood days at the pleasure I had from reading Jack London's two dog books, *White Fang* and *Call of the Wild,* both of which were set in North America. After much pondering I decided to emulate these books but featuring Horses and set in Australia.

So I started on *Fury, Son of the Wilds*. I wrote it umpteen times and got precisely nowhere. Eventually it landed up on the desk of an elderly agent. He said he would try to find a publisher for me but that my grammar was appalling and it was time I learned some proper English. If he did manage to sell, I would have to take a reduced royalty because so much work would have to be done on the typescript. A lot of this was totally over my head because I just did not know how the publishing business worked. I was also working full-time and running a home and there are only so many hours in the week.

He went ahead and sold *Fury* to Harrap, a wonderful old firm which sadly no longer exists, having been gobbled up by Chambers, although there was no sign of a takeover at the time and my book came out. Again, I was thrilled beyond measure and explanation. When a person has suffered and received enough rejection slips to paper the wall of a large room, actual success is difficult to take in – and success there was to be with this book. Eventually it would sell in America, become a school reader in Australia and be translated into a number of languages as well as coming out in paperback with Armada. Perhaps, with hindsight, I did too well for a first book, because I was still so horribly ignorant about protocol and the profession of writing itself. It would take time to absorb everything, to understand what rights can be sold with a book and generally how to go about matters. I and the agent did not last long. I believe today it is called a personality clash. In the end I thought 'what the hell' and decided to go it alone, which I did.

Many people claim that they are going to write a book but most fail to do so because they have no idea what is involved. The writing of the book itself is hard enough, with many drafts, but that is only the start of it. Finding a publisher who is prepared to invest money in the work is considerably more difficult. It takes time to make a book and there is always a question. Will somebody else produce something similar? For a start the publisher has to slot book X into his schedule because if he is any good at his job he is bringing out more than one book. He has to decide many details. What size font? What about illustrations of the cover? There will be a printer to be engaged and he too has a schedule to run a profitable business so work with him has to be slotted in. The same applies to the warehouse where the book is to be stored. How many copies in the run? How many pallets will be needed to be ordered on which the books are to be stored? How much space in the warehouse is going to be necessary for the pallets at how much rental? These are just some of a publisher's problems, all of which have to be dealt with. As to the actual book itself, has it been written on a manual typewriter, a computer; is it on floppy disk or on CD-ROM? What is the actual condition of the typescript? How much work is needed on it, grammatically and editing? Which member of staff will deal with this? Who are going to be the sub-editors? There is then the very important matter of doing the proofing to make sure it's perfect for typesetting. Errors which have to be altered by printers just about require payment in gold bars. It is possible to be printed overseas in a country like India but the problems there might be political which could cause delivery delays. Shipping the books back to this country is another. Getting the freighter with the books into the port for unloading with a fervent prayer there is not a queue for this. These are just some other stages and problems dealt with by a publisher about which an ignorant writer, through lack of knowledge, gets very impatient. From taking the book's typescript to producing the book on the shop shelves there is an awful lot of work and aggravation. When the book does finally sit snugly and proudly on the bookshelf, after the representative has been round to all the shops, twisting arms to buy, many people can only emit giant sighs of relief.

The publishing world today is a vastly different one to that of those decades ago when it was considered a very suitable occupation for a gentleman. Today, I sometimes think it is more suited to that of a cutthroat pirate.

It has changed beyond recognition from when I started and not necessarily for the better either. Many most reputable and old firms have been taken over, gobbled up my larger sharks. Those who do remain have to be financially sound indeed in these difficult economic times. Both America and Germany have moved into the British publishing scene and changed it irrevocably. As far as overseas translations are concerned there is an awful lot of piracy going on especially in a country like China. For an author to protect himself there it means the enormous hassle of engaging and working with a local lawyer.

When I started out with my first book I was totally ignorant, which was understandable, but after 50 years I consider

I know a bit about it all now. I can understand quite a few other problems from the publisher's point of view.

With all the upheaval in the book world there have been staff cutbacks, editors playing musical chairs with other firms and the general uproar of the IT age. There is also the point that writing is a very lonely occupation. A writer does not work in an office full of people where he can stop for a cup of tea and chitchat. The writer works in solitary aloofness and can indeed be very lonely because *homo sapiens* is really a herd animal.

Some books take many years to write, during which there is no income unless the writer is famous and has been able to negotiate an advance for living expenses; very rare. The mortgage and all the other domestic bills still have to be paid so for the average writer his art is a part-time occupation after he's finished his day job. There are probably no more than a handful of writers in Britain capable of producing sufficient income to be full-time at their craft.

All this I had to learn the hard way, which is no bad thing because one certainly does not forget.

When I was a young girl, as mentioned before, I was a voracious reader. I wanted to read about horses and the activities of young adults connected with them. I read a few pony books but was bitterly disappointed in them. Read one and you had read the lot. But I was particularly fond of *My Friend Flicka* and *Thunderhead, Son of Flicka* by American author Mary O'Hara; these I regarded as proper horse books.

After *Fury* came out I did some thinking. I wished to write a series of horse books with young adults and many appropriate adventures. I reviewed all the various aspects of equestrianism with which I had been involved in those days long ago when I had to work so hard for slave wages and decided to invent the Leysham Stud, placed somewhere in Britain without being specific, as this was unnecessary. My main characters were going to be a female in her late teens and an equally young male. I decided to avoid ardent love scenes because the main characters would have four legs and a mane. The human characters might even be considered incidental. This took many weeks of thought and mental debate. I made a few sketchy notes of names, ages, character and temperament. I have never been one for going into very detailed notes except later on in life when I had moved on to historical thrillers under another name. Here my historical accuracy would have to be vital and the notes I then made were more copious but more as memory reminders. Fortunately, I have always had a pretty good memory and even all those years later I have only turned to have these notes in a kind of perfunctory way, to me check on my good memory.

This work was not necessary for the series of horse books which I now planned and which would take quite a few years at one book per year with Harrap as long as they wanted me. I presumed they would if sales held up because it is very true there is no sentiment in business. A publishing firm cannot allow this. Neither could I.

I then happened to meet someone who introduced me to a third-party of great interest. He had a horse which required exercising on a regular basis and I jumped at the chance to do this. It was great to get back into the saddle again and I thoroughly enjoyed myself until the man, a farmer, moved elsewhere. But my ability had spread and I was given another opportunity to ride on a regular basis for the same reason for another fairly local family.

At the same time I had become thoroughly disillusioned with my job and left. Roy was much more settled than me. I had to get some kind of work so, being full of cheek as usual, I walked up to a garage, showed them my clean driving licence for motorbikes as well as cars, explained that I had learned to drive on a 2-ton lorry, and did they want a driver?

They didn't, but they knew someone who did. A car dealer in Bristol wanted a driver to go up to Birmingham and bring back new one-ton Land Rovers. The pay wasn't bad at all so I leapt at this offer, which intrigued me. I was given my red and white trade plates plus the train fare from Bristol to Birmingham. This went straight into my pocket; I walked up to the nearest main road, stood on the curb with my trade plates displayed prominently and started thumbing for a lift. It was dead simple and much safer than it might be today. I never had the slightest trouble getting a lift straight through to Birmingham then another one to the car manufacturers.

They came to know me very well indeed because I did this job for well over half a year. I have always liked driving and the large Land Rover did not throw me at all. I was now getting the benefit of a having learned to drive on a big lorry. It was simply a case of driving down to the Bristol showrooms, handing over the vehicle and the paperwork then going home with a generous sum of money in my pocket.

I did this for nearly a year but Roy was not at all happy about me driving in the winter months to come and especially if there should be a lot of fog so I left. Instead I went to an employment agency. I had learned to type but I was not very good really. Roy had received a commercial education and apart from his shorthand was an excellent touch typist. I was of the hunt-and-peck variety but I could get there without being too long winded in the process. I had to take some tests and answer a long battery of questions before being finally accepted.

I ended up being sent here there and everywhere when staff were required to cover for holidays and sickness. It is a peculiar position being a temp. Deep down one is neither fish, flesh nor fowl. One works for a firm but as a temp is not part and parcel of it. Some of the permanent office workers looked down their snotty noses at the humble temps but we were, after all, only earning our living. I soon learned to cut these snobs dead.

At home I was persisting with my writing so life was rather busy but enjoyable except we were not too enthusiastic about where we lived. We began chatting about another little place, preferably one in the countryside with a much larger garden and we even began gently looking around. Of course, the cottages we liked were those for which we simply could not afford the mortgage repayments and those we could afford were places we faulted for a variety of reasons.

By now my parents were home and established again and they thought we were slightly mad at our ambition for a little cottage in the country but we were a different generation and had experienced so much more.

Roy had been in the Royal Navy during the war, first as a gunner, and a good one too, then as a writer, because of his good shorthand. Upon demobilization he had joined the police service. If both of us had stayed in Britain and not ventured onto that liner it would have been impossible for us to meet. Our lifestyles had nothing whatsoever in common. I have often wondered if other couples also met on the liner *New Australia*. There is a corny old saying that shipboard romances never last. They only resemble ships passing in the night. Rubbish!

We finally found a cottage at Lower Common in South Gloucestershire, which we could just afford. It was small but had potential. There was about one acre of land with it, although it was in a dreadful condition as pigs had been roaming there. After much thought about our financial situation and consultation with our building society we put our semi-detached house up for sale and decided to take the plunge. It was 10 miles from where Roy worked so at some time in the future he would have to try to obtain a more local position at the nearby new town of Yate, built to provide housing for people after the dreadful Bristol Blitzs.

In fact, Yate is very ancient indeed. It is down in the Domesday Book as either 'Giete' or 'Gete' (the spelling depends upon William I's clerks).

William I obviously had a very suspicious mind and did not entirely trust anybody. After his conquest of Britain in 1066 he decided he wanted to know exactly what his victory had given him and decided to have everything counted, checked and written down in the Domesday Book. He sent his educated clerks out on the mission to count everything: people, animals, poultry, food, wine and all goods as well as that most important asset – land. Once the first lot of clerks had gone on their merry way, obedient to a King who was known to be utterly ruthless when provoked, William sent out a second lot of clerks to check on the first! These two lots of clerks have caused confusion to historians because their spelling was not consistent. This is why the old Norman name for Yate is found spelled in two different ways.

It was one of these spelling variations that I would, many decades later, utilize for my own benefit when I decided to self-publish. I had to have a name and plucked Giete out of the air.

Chapter XI

We moved into our little Jasmine Cottage and had an immediate crisis on our hands. For a long time Roy had wanted a pet, a cat with a bright blue eyes, a Siamese. I was not at all certain about this because I had been brought up with dogs, but we started investigating in the Bristol area. To our surprise there was not one Siamese ready or available for us and we ended up purchasing a kitten from Kent. It was out of the question for me to drive there when we had just moved house and were in a real pickle. We arranged for the breeder to take the kitten under personal escort to London and put her on the train at Paddington. So far so good.

We went down to Bristol Temple Meads to collect our kitten but she was not there. We waited for train after train from London to no avail so drove back to our cottage after first sending a telegram to the breeder. "Where is our kitten?" the telephone had not yet been connected so communication was very difficult.

We had not been back for an hour when a strange female came stamping up the drive, wearing a mask of fury on her face. When we opened the door she demanded to know the reason for our behaviour in not collecting our kitten from Temple Meads railway station.

To say we were taken aback is a mild explanation for our mood as we protested and explained we had just come back from the station where all knowledge of any kitten was denied. I hastily refilled a hot water bottle and we drove as fast as possible back to Temple Meads. I was very uneasy by now, remembering the utter fiasco taking those two horses to Skegness.

We arrived at Temple Meads to an absolute uproar. An inspector from the R.S.P.C.A had been down and told them if the kitten wasn't found, alive and well, he would close the place down.

The kitten was found and produced in her little travelling basket and looked absolutely fed up, which was not surprising. She had been travelling all day from Kent, no food, no water and no litter tray. She had been there all the time we had waited previously. I hastily shoved the hot water bottle into the basket and she cuddled up to it. Then it was back to the cottage as quickly as possible. I told myself this appeared to be typical of the railways when it came to moving animals and never again would I become part of such a disgraceful situation. I wouldn't trust the railways to move an insect. This was my second horrible experience and we were lucky this little kitten had been tough enough to survive.

That is how we acquired our first feline pet, who we called Tao. She was to live with us for fourteen incredible years, during which time I became irrevocably hooked on having a cat as a pet. They can become enormously close to a person and can be remarkably entertaining with their fads and foibles and, very gradually, I began to prefer them to dogs. Even my father, a dyed-in-the-wool dog man, fell under her spell, which was a remarkable event in itself.

I was still involved with my writing but because of these domestic circumstances it had become a bit hit and miss. I had produced nine books with the dear old house of Harrap. As I had planned so long ago, each dealt with a different aspect of equestrianism and with plenty of adventures. One of my favourites was called *Jago* and I dedicated this, like *Fury*, to Roy. It was the opposite theme to the latter and I felt satisfied I had done what I set out to do all those years ago.

Now what though? I had said everything I had to say with regard to horse books for children and felt it was now time to move on and stretch my wings with adult books. I felt confident enough to consider this because my Leysham Stud series with Harrap had done very well indeed. They had been translated into German, Danish, Dutch, Portuguese and Afrikaans – the latter of which astonished me and I had a good relationship with the publisher, of about 10 years' duration. But I had to move on because I knew it was time. I felt it in my bones. But on what subject? I was drawn to British history, especially before the Norman Conquest but I was acutely aware that a lot of research would be necessary and, of course, this was in the days long before computers and the internet, which have made research of this kind so much easier and possible to do from home.

At our new home we started to tackle the jungle of a garden, which had hedges that appeared to be yards thick from lack of maintenance. It was extremely hard physical labour but we thrived on it. There was something most satisfying in licking this piece of land into a shape to suit us. There was a fair amount of grass to cut plus flowerbeds and a large vegetable patch to be tended.

At the bottom, on one corner, we left a piece solely to nature because it was here we would have bonfires to burn all the rubbish and use the ashes to feed the soil. I found this latter portion of the garden of very deep interest. I would sit there, absolutely quiet and still and watch the wildlife as it went about its business. Very gradually the animals, birds and insects accepted me like a permanent fixture. Across this piece of land, from one side to the other, was a well used fox's road and they were incredibly bold. They would step through the hedge, give me a long thoughtful look, then trot across as if they owned the place. It was most comical to watch.

'Write about only that which you know' is the author's mantra, so I wrote a book about a miners' strike. It was between 60 and 70,000 words long and I offered it to Harrap, who promptly turned it down. Feeling a little deflated, I offered it elsewhere and, at the same time, started one called

Copper, about the police. I had learned a lot about them from Roy and we had both becomes special constables. We used to go on duty every Saturday afternoon and evening and tried to do our bit as citizens. Gradually it stopped feeling strange because I was always sent out with Roy who, as an ex constable from Leeds, knew all there was to know about it. We did this part-time voluntary work for three years, then father died.

It all happened very suddenly. Bob had been down to visit us through a weekend and father had met him at his door and said, "I don't think I have long to go." I didn't learn about this until later. He went to bed in his normal good health and hadn't been lying down half an hour when his body gave a few violent jerks and he died. Just like that.

Someone came with a telephone message and we rushed over there in the middle of the night. Naturally, I was most distressed. It was a sad time and it became obvious that life was going to have to change because Mother was not in the best of health. With hindsight it was amazing she had lived so long because she had always had breathing problems and was a bronchial asthmatic. It would be out of the question for her to stay alone in a semi-detached house with stairs and again, looking back, they should have put in for a pensioner's bungalow years before. It is so easy to be wise after the event.

Roy had suggested that they have a residential caravan on our huge piece of land which purchase was on the point of going through.

I had obtained a summer job at a garden centre which I found of great interest and learned all about taking cuttings, planting on and the mysteries of the pH content of the soil. This was all strange to me and I soaked up knowledge like the proverbial sponge but the job was only for the summer and autumn.

At the same time Roy was on the verge of changing his job so what with one thing and another we resigned our positions as special constables. We had done our bit for well over three years but life looked as if it was going to move on in one of those violent jerks.

I sent my miners book out again and again but each time it bounced back with appalling regularity. I continued writing my book on the police force and went up to the Gloucester-shire Forces' headquarters where I met the Chief Constable and many other male and female officers. I was given free rein to question all of them but as I carried on with writing this work, I also became distinctly uneasy.

Did these rejections mean I was unsatisfactory as an adult writer? This thought stuck in my throat because I did not want to go back to writing horse books again. They were well and truly out of my system. I had said all that could be said without being repetitive and boring. I had also begun to have the feeling that Harrap was changing the tone of the books they were publishing. They had done very well out of my books but publishers must move on to bring in the profit. I had no idea that in the near future they would vanish as a publishing house in a takeover. Such a possibility had never occurred to me. Today, of course, such events are common-place, and not just with publishers but any business. I think they call it progress.

I did some researching and wrote a historical saga, *Land and Power*, which I send to an agent. She agreed to try it and this was finally accepted by Robert Hale, a long-established independent publisher. I was very pleased when they accepted it and the contract arrived, which did wonders for my rather deflated morale.

I then did something totally different, which quite fasci-nated me. I wrote a book called *The Law of the Wild*, based solely upon my observations of our piece of garden we had left totally wild. This was quite difficult to write because there would not be a human being in it nor one word of dialogue, of course. I made each chapter cover roughly a month and the whole book, although only about 45,000 words, would describe a year in the lives of the natural inhabitants as they went about their activities. There had to be a central character but I gave it two: a magnificent tree and a bold fox. Everything would revolve around the area in which the tree stood and where the fox had his earth. All the other living creatures would be tied into this small area.

Although everything had been observed by me there were certain details I had to check and recheck at Yate library. Like for example, exactly how did a spider make its web? How did the weather conditions affect the wild creatures if there was a cold wet spell, or long dry one? I wrote this book from my heart and it became one of my great favourites. It was sold and then published by Rex Collings. This gentleman publisher is long deceased and his company with him. Right now I have the workout for consideration for republishing with another house just as I have with my children's horse books. *Nature's Law*, as I call it, now has a delightful foreword from Professor David Bellamy, who read and liked it very much.

It was not really satisfactory having a frail lady like Mother in the caravan and at the same time we were getting itchy feet again. From the very practical angle Roy pointed out that we would not be able to manage this amount of land and keep it as we liked with the passing of years, so we started looking around again for a more urban property. Finally we found a suitable house, another semi-detached, but on the outskirts of Yate's residential area. We sold the cottage and Mother's caravan and she would come to live with us until the council had provided her with a downstairs flat somewhere.

Deep down, I was very distressed as the furniture lorry arrived and we took our leave of our little cottage because we had been very happy there. Roy was correct though. It would have been heart-breaking to see our lovely garden go to rack and ruin because we could not maintain it in our old age.

It was another almighty upheaval and the most astonished of all was Tao. From having a giant country garden she would have to make do with the semi's average plot but she was well into middle age and would adapt. There was a main road within 100 yards so we prudently fenced in our back garden because Tao knew nothing about traffic and its dangers. It also gave us privacy.

Once we had everything in place and all the boxes removed we turned our attention to this small back garden, which resembled a tip and even included half of a tree trunk. There was much to'ing and fro'ing as all that rubbish was removed and we settled down with our spades during our spare time.

I had obtained work at a private employment bureau which I found a great interest interviewing the applicants for work as well as the firms who had vacancies. This job lasted for one year but never made a great amount of money so closed. I was offered a small office job as the clerk but I knew from past experience shuffling bits of paper would drive me up the wall.

I was still messing about with my writing and that is the operative word. I did not quite know what I wanted to do nor how. The miners and police typescripts were put to one side and eventually I came to consider them as simply a learning exercise and shredded them. Looking back now I did the right thing, not just because of my writing but mostly because the market was inappropriate.

I still had it in mind to write historical books but not simple love stories. I loved to read action books and this was what I wished to do. At the same time I was totally uninterested in writing about the kings and queens of old because their lives had been covered by so many other authors. When I would be ready to start I wish to write about how history affected the ordinary people of the period in question.

Chapter XII

Mother was settled in a decent ground floor flat and Grandma Bullen was long deceased. Mother's brothers had also died as well as many people on Roy's side of his family. It was simply the natural march of time.

In my daydreaming moments I had often thought it would be lovely to travel again but those wistful dreams were always quickly buried because they took time and money. I simply could not see how we would ever have the wherewithal to indulge this fancy. We had already done the usual trips to France, Austria and Germany and with our voyages to and from Australia we had seen a great chunk of the world, far more than the average.

When I was in my early teens I had decided I would like a pen-friend and my old school arranged this. My pen-friend was a Czech girl one year older than myself and we had corresponded, on and off, over the years. It would be wonderful to meet her but at this time Czechoslovakia, as it was then called, was very much a hard line communist country. I did discuss taking a chance and going over there for a week with a lady from Austria who knew more about the situation than myself. She strongly advised me to forget this idea in the current political climate. It was not that she thought there would be danger to me over there, but more from the point of safety for Alex and her family. I took note of what she said and did exactly nothing although I was very circumspect in the comments I made in my letters. I bent over backwards to make no political statement but to keep my letters very light and airy. At the same time I decided one day I would go over there but obviously the time was not ripe.

Roy saw a job advertised which caught his eye and we discussed it. He applied with his shorthand typing ability and we were taken aback when he was accepted by the BAC at Preston Lancashire. The work was in Saudi Arabia at the Royal Saudi Air Force Base at Tabuk in the north of that country. What appealed to both of us was that the remuneration was not only generous but tax-free provided the man did not come back and spent more than six weeks in this country in any one year. It would be a big step because I would be left here alone with Tao. I certainly would not leave Mother because she had started to go downhill pretty rapidly. Indeed, I knew it was remarkable she had lived so long because there were so much wrong with her, now including a swollen heart.

Roy's engagement was for a single man originally but once he had been there for a specific period I could have gone over and joined him. Apart from Mother and our cherished Tao, who was far too old to re-home, I did not fancy living in such a strict Arab country. I had read just a little too much and not just about Lawrence of Arabia either. Saudi Arabia is a strict Moslem country at the centre of the Islamic faith and has the holy cities of Mecca and Medina. Infidel white tourists there were neither wanted nor allowed. It was also very strange to realize Roy was going to work in a country which we had twice passed on our voyages to and from Australia. Life can certainly be very queer indeed.

I kept picking up little office jobs and then I decided to go quite mad and take a correspondence course for educational reasons. I was a long way from schooldays at 14 years but even I never envisaged how difficult it was going to be. Learning on a correspondence course is every bit as lonely an occupation as writing a book. I found it all enormously hard and then came the crunch time of sitting for an examination. I had decided to cut my teeth with an O-level, as it was then called, in English. To take the examination I had to sit at the local school with all the children and felt rather old against them. To my astonishment I passed with an A grade.

This encouraged me so I decided to do a bit more and enrolled for three A-levels in law, politics and history. I was disappointed with the latter. I have always been particularly interested in the history of this country before 1066. The period I was given was the 17th Century, about which I knew nothing and I was not greatly enthusiastic but that was the period chosen for that year, take it or leave it.

I found A level reading very difficult by correspondence. I would come across a problem and write to my tutor about it but it could take three weeks to get a reply. I would not advise anyone to study this way because ultimately it can be totally demoralizing.

At this point, of course, all my writing had been put well and truly on the backburner. I had too much work to do at home for these studies as well as keep an eye on Mother and visit very regularly indeed. I wrote each day a diary letter to Roy, which was posted once a week. Letters were of tremendous importance to the men in that country but theirs only came out once a week. Friday was the day in which the week started leave and was that on which men came home. A responsible man was always given the task of taking the mail for Britain and posting it at Heathrow. This says rather a lot for the Saudi postal system!

I missed Roy so desperately and him me but it was all a means to an end and we would ultimately benefit financially and perhaps even manage to do the travelling about which we had often talked.

My life was very full and quite hectic. With considerable trepidation I went back to the school to sit the A-level examinations held both morning and afternoon. I had no confidence at all and when the results came out this was justified, I did pass but my grades were low, two D and one E, nothing to get excited about except they were passes.

Then, for one of the few times in my life, I let myself be brainwashed into going further into higher education. By this time Roy was in Arabia and the leave allocation was one day for each week over there. Men were allowed home on leave every 15 weeks so we had some precious time together. On one of the leaves Roy expressed a wish to go north to see the few remaining members of his family so we dropped Mother off with some distant cousins while Tao had to go into a cattery. Roy's leave flew by with horrendous speed and all too soon he was off again.

My brainwashing consisted of a lady solicitor friend telling me to apply to the polytechnic,10 miles away, now known as the University of the West of England or UWE. I thought the idea too crazy for words but she nibbled away at me so eventually I did apply for the law degree course. I had a nasty feeling I was wasting my time but it would be a new experience if nothing else.

I turned up and, after wandering around like a lost soul, I eventually managed to find where I was supposed to go. What an eye-opener! I was the oldest person there, just about the decrepit granny, while the rest were avid teenagers from sixth form. To start with I felt very uncomfortable but the youngsters were very good. They absorbed me into their camaraderie and I even began to enjoy myself but I still had considerable doubt about my learning ability since I am not academic.

There were four subjects: contracts, torts, legal history and constitutional law. Parts of the subjects of the latter two interested me enormously, but I struggled. There was so much reading to do as well as work to hand in after we had attended the lecture theatre and seminars. I was still running our home, seeing Mother three times a week to take her out and for her shopping and library books, as well as writing to Roy each day – which I never once missed in what was to be six years. I should not have been trying to study in the first place. After two months I realized this, but stuck it out, although I had a sneaking feeling the first year examinations would be my downfall.

How correct I was! I passed three subjects but failed torts by four marks. I was entitled to re-sit for consideration to go on into year two but this time I failed by six marks. I received the message loud and clear. Once I was over my initial disappointment, my lady solicitor friend started on me again for the last time. She said I should apply to go on the legal executive associate course. There were four subjects there but I could claim exemption from one because of the exams I had passed, even though they were of low grade. Tuition was on one day a week only in Bristol but to go on the course the student had to prove they were working in a legal practice; without this, they were not accepted.

I thought about it all then went and saw another solicitor whom I knew and for whom, in the last couple of years, I had done temp work as a typist as well as attending the courts as his clerk to wait on his barrister. This latter work was of particular interest but it was only temporary. I told him my whole story and between us it was decided I would go in his offices every morning to do whatever had to be done and I would refuse payment. This was quite okay by me and it suited him of course because the work would not be arduous and it gave me some more precious free time with my domestic commitments as well.

So once again I started on the merry-go-round of belated studying. It was still difficult because of my circumstances but I pushed on willy-nilly. Then it was exam time once more and this time I felt a little bit more confident. With justification. I passed all the exams then completely ran out of steam. Someone suggested I should do another three years to obtain a fellowship, which would equal a degree. I did not want to know now. Such education should be undertaken with a free mind and not the moral obligations with which I had to live.

When Roy had been in Arabia for two years he was entitled for me to go out to visit him for a fortnight at company expense. I wanted to go very much but I was worried about leaving Mother for such a time. However, a member of the family stepped in and she went to stay with them for the two weeks, which removed an awful lot of my worries. It wasn't possible then to telephone direct to the base at Tabuk. The drill was to ring the head office at Wharton in Lancashire and they would radio messages over. Each wife had a man for her welfare, someone to whom she could always turn in times of trouble or emergencies. I found it an excellent system.

I flew into Jeddah and the hot and extremely humid heat really hit me and almost took me back to Brisbane days. I then had to change to the domestic flight but there were some other men coming back off leave who took me under their wing.

We did not fly direct but had to land at Wedj, a very small desert place where the local sheik had stated he wanted a plane – now! From there it was onto Tabuk, where Roy met me. On the previous leave he had warned me, no hugging or kissing – not in Saudi Arabia. We greeted each other with a cool handshake which would have pleased even the strictest of their religious police!

A lot of rubbish has been written about this country. There have also been comments, not always complimentary, many of which are true. These are different people with a culture totally unlike ours. It is also the birthplace of Osama bin Laden. Although now banned in his own country after 9/11 he still has connections there and the Saudis themselves have had terrorist problems. They are particularly vulnerable with the oil pipelines from their wells, which are especially difficult to guard completely, over a vast distance and under that roasting sun. I had thought I knew all about heat from my previous experiences but this was something different, quite out of this world. When outside it was as if a person has stepped right into a roasting hot oven with very dry heat.

When flying over this country it is quite easy to pick out the winding beds of dried up rivers. In certain parts there are enormous sand dunes and one area is called the Empty Quarter, which name speaks for itself. Not all the desert has brown sand like that at Blackpool. Some of it is a powdery, dismal grey.

There are some very rich people in that country, to whom money is no object at all. I learned later that the planes which fly from the Royal Saudi base at Tabuk were almost nothing but a flying club for the rich Princes. The Saudis, quite rightly, wanted their own version of the British RAF but this was easier said than done. The people who did the groundwork, the mechanics and fitters, were often ordinary people inducted into positions which they didn't want in the first place. Before they could be taught anything they had to learn English.

The Bedu were the genuine desert people who lived in large black tents and who roamed with their animals as and where the fancy took them over the Bondu, as the desert was familiarly called.

Roy worked in the school where lessons were arranged and held for often very reluctant and even resentful pupils. It appeared they had a long way to go before they had their own version of the RAF and its ground staff but they had their oil revenue to pay for all this as well as the very best planes possible.

It may be remembered only a certain while ago, when Tony Blair was Prime Minister, investigations into bribery were hastily smothered on the grounds of national security. More likely it was because we would have lost an incredible order for planes which would simply have gone elsewhere. There are many questions still to be answered on this point but I wonder if they ever will be?

While I was there Roy was given fairly generous time off, only working half days, so he was able to take me out and about. I was not allowed to drive a car as a female but large cars were going from the base into the town all the time. I never had any trouble in the towns with the Arabs. Indeed, I felt a lot safer there than I would be walking around one of our English towns at night in this 21st century.

Another point I noticed, when in town with Roy, a female always walked directly behind her man. Me do that? Not likely! I am far too Anglo Saxon. I walked alongside him as I would do in this country but naturally never took his hand or arm. The religious police would have been disgusted with that. When we walked down one of their scruffy pavements towards a group of Arabs there would be energetic activity from them as they made sure they did not even touch me with a sleeve.

Nevertheless, it was one more of these wonderful experiences through which I have been lucky to live, although we were getting rather fed up with the separation. As they say in good old Yorkshire, "brass isn't the be all and end all of life."

We talked about it and decided one more year and that would be it. I was not going to have any more of educating myself but to turn back to my writing. I had lots of ideas and a beaten-up manual typewriter. It would be up to me to get everything down in print and take it from there. Computers are everywhere now but at this time they were so scarce they were objects to study rather than use. Only large firms could afford them and they were hulking great brutes. Today when one sees a neat little laptop it is quite startling how technology has zoomed ahead, probably faster than at any time before in Man's existence. I have not quite decided whether this is a good or bad thing because not everything old was fit to be trashed. Some of the old ways were good, reliable, trustworthy and decent.

We flew back to Britain again as Roy had arranged this to coincide with one of his leaves and in his eyes it was wonderful to see green grass, clouds and even feel rain. We relaxed and enjoyed each other's company. Roy particularly liked the ability to go out to have a pint of beer and eat bacon sandwiches as well as pork crackling, all forbidden under Islam. Then it was time for him to go again and we faced one more year's separation.

I had one final trip out there. Roy told the base commander he had had enough and wished to leave so I went out for this last trip. I was deeply worried about Mother but she was determined not to hold me back and I arranged many people to call and see her on a daily basis, which they did.

This time I knew where I was going and what to expect. Roy had arranged for someone to provide a car and take us out so I could see the Bondu properly. This was another incredible day. We had a kind of picnic with us and plenty of fluid to drink and the air-conditioner in the car worked flat out to keep us cool. We pulled up at one place and I stepped out and saw the distinct winding track of quite a large snake. I decided it was prudent to stay near the car.

Then we came to a place where there were swimmers in that part of the sea but men only of course. The females in that land don't have much of a life in my opinion. I thought I had seen cruel scenery before in Australia in the dry bush but it was nothing compared to this. What met my eyes was a lack of colour; everywhere was brown or grey, although I spotted some deep red and green rocks. These arose from the ores of copper and tin. It would seem this country has been generously endowed with mineral as well as oil wealth. There were a few huge bustards in the sky; large, clumsy-looking birds with a big wingspan.

The extreme heat plus the wind and sometimes quite cold nights had, over the centuries, cut and gouged some nearby mountains to make them jagged and awesome. In the clear, unpolluted air, everything stood out in sharp relief and seemingly near yet in reality was a long distance away.

The only people we saw in the desert were the Bedu, with their large black tents and females dressed in this colour as well. With them would be their wealth in the form of camels and goats. Probably they may be some of the freest people in the world but for how long? Will modern technology catch up with them? Will someone tried to bully them to live in urban areas? Every country has very stupid people.

When we returned I did not like the look of Mother or the fact the doctor called weekly of his own accord. I later found out Mother had sworn him to confidentiality and secrecy. Unknown to me she had breast cancer and was in her 80th year. Surgery was out of the question for two reasons. One she refused point-blank to be cut up again and secondly she would have died on the table with a grossly swollen heart.

By this time, after much thought, we had decided to come out of a freehold property and rent instead. We negotiated the tenancy of a flat in a shopping centre. Many of our 'circle' thought we were stark raving mad but we knew we were doing the right thing.

We were well into middle age and without children or close family of any kind, just distant cousins, all of whom were well-heeled, so we decided to let somebody else have the cost of the repairs. When the time was right we would do the travelling which we fancied.

For a little while, until the Inland Revenue began sniffing around, we visited a few local offices, installed pot plants and then, once a week, went round and attended to them. It was nothing but a little paying hobby, it got us out without going far and there were something very satisfactory in turning a dull office into somewhere most pleasant for people to go. Plants have enormous therapeutic value and we had many compliments about our displays.

I used to go to Mother every other day and would ring morning and night without fail. I rang one morning and the phone was not answered. We raced over there and I managed to unfasten the safety chain so we could get in. She was on the floor and I never did find out how long she had been there. The ambulance men got her up quickly and took her to the nearby hospital. It was here the doctor took me to one side and told me about the breast cancer. I was totally aghast at her secrecy, obviously done to save me from fretting. Within a week she had died and was at peace. Right to the end there was no word of complaint from her and she died as she had lived, a tough little Yorkshire tyke.

I was enormously distressed because although we were heading towards our old age slowly, when the last parent does die it signifies an end of an era. Something had gone for all time. I had known her for exactly 53 years. Mother was in her 80th year so she herself would have been the first to admit she had a pretty good innings.

Chapter XIII

The film star Bette Davis made a most profound remark which made us think. "Old age ain't for cissies!" and how right she was. I also remembered what Mother had said many months ago, quite out of the blue.

"Get out and about while you can, you don't know how you will end up. I never thought I'd end up like this!"

Upon reflection, perhaps she was like my father. She knew what was going to happen. I am just so thankful she didn't have to lie in a hospital bed for a long time in total misery.

We decided to go to Russia and the country was then Communist. We flew to Moscow and as we approached for the landing I peered through the window and looked down upon a landscape of silver birch trees. It was August and still daylight and they made the most wonderful sight. I have never been able to look at a silver birch tree since without thinking of that city.

It was a kind of organized tour; obviously the Communists did not want many people from Britain wandering around their country poking their noses in where they shouldn't. The main part of the holiday was to be nearly three days on that incredible feat of engineering, the Trans Siberian railway. An awesome construction when a person considers the vast distances involved, the hostile terrain and above all their winter climate. We had read about it before we left home.

We had two days in Moscow and lodged in a superb hotel. On each floor there was a babushka female with eyes like laser rays who did not miss a thing we did. There were people outside the hotel entrance too, men in suits, and they were not there for decoration either. We had suspected it would be like this and were not at all upset by it. If they wished to think we were all James Bond that was their problem.

We did some gentle exploring then had to go to the airport again to fly to eastern Siberia to board the train. We flew to Khabarovsk and it was quite remarkable. As we were going exactly east it was a non-stop dawn so by the time we arrived we both felt a bit fragile because it was a long flight. We all know Russia is the largest country in the world but this vastness cannot be fully appreciated until one starts to fly over it. The land just goes on and on and on.

The Trans-Siberian railway runs from Moscow to Vladivostok, which is the terminus. As Westerners we were not allowed into Vladivostok because it was a restricted area, something to do with their naval fleet, we guessed, so we boarded our train the next stop up the line of any size.

The compartments were for four people; we shared with a couple who were our own age and we all got on very well. There were roughly 26 of us in the group and we were all in one train compartment, not scattered through the train where we would be difficult to watch and certainly not allowed to mix with the ordinary passengers. At the end of each compartment was a cubbyhole and in there lived two ancient babushkas. Their prized possession was an enormous samovar, about which they were rather possessive. This samovar was to provide us with tea, night or day and very good it was too. No milk or sugar but they were irrelevant details. Tea drunk straight from a samovar has its own unique flavour and we thought it quite delicious. These ladies also had a stove which was kept going night and day and which provided warmth for the whole coach. We thought them a delightful couple even if we did not have one word of language between us.

Our meals were to be taken en masse in another coach from which the ordinary travellers were banned. This had been coupled next to our day and night coach so there was no chance to do any wandering at all.

It was a corridor carriage and there was no objection to us strolling up and down this to take in the scenery. At the various stations we were allowed off the train to wander around the platforms and take in the local sights and sounds. Here our two babushkas really came into their own. They changed from being tea makers to sheepdogs. Each carried a little coloured flag. As we dismounted onto the platforms they would wave these at us. When it was time to board again there were more waves and the two old dears bustled around behind us, anxiously shooing us back onto 'their' train. It was all rather comical but also touching. While we were travelling in their compartment on that train we were their possessions to be guarded and protected fiercely. We went out of our way to be obliging, courteous, and, most of all, obedient. We did not wish for these two bosomy ancients to be carted off to some dreadful gulag because of our conduct.

Some of the stops were for half an hour, which gave us plenty of time to wander around. One or two individuals from our group – there are always stupid ones – tried to leave the station, obviously to rubberneck. They were soon dragged, just about by the scruff of their necks, and flung unceremoniously back into the coach. Serve them right too.

The important stops were at Chita for Harbin and China and Ulan Ude for the capital of Mongolia Ulaanbaatar. We had plenty of time to wander around the platform and look at everything while the locals studied us in turn. We all exchanged smiles with each other but that was as far as fraternization went when we had no language between us.

At all of these stations where we had a longish halt, we were entertained by another crowd of aged babushkas who appeared seemingly from nowhere. They proved to be ardent capitalists who knew the value of every rouble and kopeck!

They had small trestle tables, which they hastily erected, and all the Russian travellers made an instant beeline for these old dears. Soon there was a crowd around each table and we could not, for the life of us, work out the attraction, so we joined the crowd and shuffled forward, eyes in all directions, until we found out what it was all about. The goods on sale, wrapped up in tatty and not too clean newspaper, folded in a certain pattern, were simply boiled potatoes. They were obviously an enormous favourite with the ordinary train travellers, who probably could not afford the dining car. It was quite an eye-opener.

The train moved steadily westwards through the taiga and we were glad that all the windows were shut. The flies and mosquitoes were quite out of this world. The weather was extremely hot outside but what fascinated me was the kaleidoscope of quite wonderful wildflowers. They were every shade and colour and were a sight to study. It would be wonderful to have got off and walked among them.

The wildlife was quite used to the train and simply ignored it so we were able watch the land animals and birds, which enthralled both of us. It was a case of looking through the window of our sleeping compartment or the window of the corridor. Either way we were on our legs for hour up on hour, only sitting down in the restaurant car for our meals. There was simply so much to see.

A lot of the land is waterlogged to the extent that many of the telegraph poles leaned in a quite drunken fashion. What was even more incredible to both of us was the way the single railway track turned because of the terrain. We would be looking through the window of our carriage in a certain direction when we would see the locomotive at the front of our train coming towards us. It was almost eerie but was caused because the rail track had to follow firm ground. Sometimes these loops were enormous, at other times relatively small. It was quite something to see.

After 2½ days we detrained at Irkutsk and were all rather unsteady on our legs. The reason we left the train here was to stay overnight and have the opportunity to visit the famous lake Baikal, the largest and deepest freshwater lake in the whole world, which still holds many marine secrets. It is such a crying shame that part of it is polluted from industrial waste. Environmental issues were considered unimportant in Soviet Russia. It is thought that one-day this lake will be able to clean itself but is going to take time. Local folklore about this lake says that if a person paddles in the lake they will live into their 80s, while full immersion just about guarantees a century of life.

From Irkutsk we flew to Bratsk in the Siberian Centre, which is a most unusual place. It was a brand new city populated only by young people when we were there. When World War II ended the Soviets decided a new city was required which must be built in the heart of the taiga. A dozen men camped in tents and made plans for the city. They also intended to build an enormous hydroelectric power station and giant dam. In this part of the world there are only 82 days in each year free from frost. That did not daunt the Soviets. They built their dam and also their city in both summer and winter by the simple method of using boiling concrete in the cold months. At first this was kept hot by electric power, which worked out rather expensive, but then someone came up with a bright idea of using the exhaust gases from the lorries that carried the concrete. No matter what weather was thrown at them – and in Siberia it can get very nasty indeed – they continued with their building.

To our surprise the Soviet guide, with excellent English, was quite open about this and we were taken to the dam and allowed inside the viewing room, which was quite an experience. We were told the greatest problem of all did not arise from the cold but from the millions of mosquitoes.

Everyone had to stay fully clothed in the heat – and it can get very hot there too – including the animals they were using. They tried everything they could think of, including all the sprays available, but it was not until the dam's waters started a backup that this problem was beaten. The rising waters simply drowned all the insects.

We flew back to Moscow through Kuybyshev, catching up on all the time zones again. We had a short couple of days there, in which we bravely tried the underground. We would get our guide to write down directions in our language and the names we wanted in the Cyrillic alphabet.

We explored Red Square and watched the very smart guards change shifts at Lenin's tomb. There was always a long queue to view his body and as Western tourists we could have gone ahead of the locals but we declined. Viewing a dead body was not our idea of fun.

Then it was back to the airport again for a flight to Leningrad, which today has reverted to its original name of St Petersburg. What a historical city this is but what a bloody past. In World War II it was under siege by the Germans for 2½ years. Citizens died in their thousands from cold, disease and starvation. No other city suffered quite so much as this one and there is a monument to show just how near to the centre the Germans did get.

It was here that the Czars had their summer Palace, which is now a superb museum. It was also the place to which starving people marched to ask to the Czar to give them bread. Instead he gave them his Cossacks with drawn sabres. The same thing happened at Odessa on those long, famous steps.

We stood quietly in the main square, where the blood of those brave men, women and children was spilled so ruthlessly. Our own Peterloo was the same, but on a much tinier scale. All over this vast land there are many burying grounds and monuments as these people pay homage for 365 days in the year. They are tough people and I like them very much indeed, which I say without any recourse to politics whatsoever.

Our holiday ended here and we flew back to Gatwick. We had seen and experienced so much that we knew we would be talking about it for many months to come.

We collected our pet cats from the cattery and settled back down again for an English winter. Tao had long gone. We had to have her put down because of cancer. No pet we own will ever suffer. I have a very strong belief in euthanasia for all living creatures (including Man) who have an incurable condition which means they live in misery.

During that winter I had a small A to Z non-fiction horse book published. Years later, when this independent publisher had ceased to exist, it would come out again with another publishing house and be more extensive. It was a good little book and aimed at those who were starting off to ride or to own a horse and lacked knowledge. It was called *The Pocket Dictionary of the Horse* and when it came out a second time with Tabb House of Cornwall the word 'revised' was simply inserted at the title. Tabb House did an excellent professional job in this publication and I was very pleased indeed and still am. My compliments to Mrs Caroline White.

Deep down I still be yearned to be published as an adult fiction writer. During all the years my friend Ann and I had kept in faithful contact and I was godmother to her younger daughter. At the same time my letter writing connections continued with my pen-friend Alexandra in Prague. Sometimes there would be ominous gaps in this correspondence and it was difficult to know what to do for her safety. Whenever I knew anyone was going into Europe I would give them a letter to post with her address. I learned later all these letters did eventually arrive with unusual European postmarks, which baffled her to start with until she worked out my ploy. So we kept in touch and I became more and more determined I was going to meet her and to hell with politics.

Until this meeting could be arranged, with total safety to her and her family, I could do nothing but mark time. The regime in power then in that particular country was rather bad. It was difficult to get information on what was happening exactly in the old Czechoslovakia and Alex could say nothing to me in her letters. We had been corresponding for decades now and had, instinctively, worked out a kind of code. When read by anyone else our sentences were completely innocuous but to us were full of a double meaning.

Later on, when more facts became available to me, I was very glad I had always been so careful. Her husband, she found out after her divorce from him, was rather high up in the old StB (secret police) and then when she married a second time he was, believe it or not, a very high ranking army colonel. I also learned, much later on, that letters from the West were not opened physically but were read by some x-ray method. There was nothing private whatsoever in our correspondence but neither was there ever anything which could jeopardize Alexandra's safety.

Chapter XIV

I spent many hours of the winter in Yate library until I was just about a permanent fixture, like one of their chairs. I was researching very seriously now on our history and gradually the librarian and staff became used to me and gave me free rein of the books that were kept locked up. This was a great help to me because there were still no computers and I wouldn't have known how to use one anyhow. Even though this book is being written on a computer I am very conscious that the more I learn about this gadget the more I have to learn and I am still wearing very large red L plates in the process.

We began to talk about where we would go to next and we both fancied seeing South Africa, even though the country was still in the grip of apartheid. I was exceedingly well read on this country because their great author Stuart Cloete was a favourite of mine. He wrote extensive fiction novels about the life of the Boers and then produced his masterpiece *Rags of Glory*. I have a copy and, for relaxation, even though just about word perfect, I always go and pick up *Rags*. Why someone has never grabbed the film rights baffles me. I consider it far superior to *Gone With the Wind*. It has more depth, more history and, with apologies to Margaret Mitchell, I consider it better written. Anyone who wants a good read should get hold of a copy.

We were to be away three weeks this time because our plan was to take in the country of Namibia, the old German South West Africa, a country about which we knew very little. We knew that this part of the vast continent produced diamonds, which could be picked up on certain beaches, making them out of bounds to everyone.

We flew down to Johannesburg and then caught a plane to Namibia on a tour that commenced at Windhoek. Roy always arranged that we go on an official tour so we would have a guide who spoke our language and knew all the interesting bits and pieces. When a couple go alone, unless they are fantastically lucky, they can miss out on so much.

After a night in a hotel we boarded the waiting coach, whose guide spoke both English and German as well as Afrikaans. How I admire people who speak many languages. I am typically useless with no talent whatsoever in this field.

We had flown over the Kalahari Desert to reach Windhoek and by now there was nothing Roy did not know about deserts and I had had my share of them as well. As we drove about, with points of interest being drawn to our attention, we found there was still a heavy German influence in the architecture. There was a railway line at Walvis Bay, which the Germans had used when they were the colonial occupying power, and one rather pathetic little tank engine.

We travelled on to the Etosha game reserve. The guard at the gate to the reserve was a San, and how smart he looked in his uniform. The San are the Bushmen of this land, very small and very tough, often with huge backsides, nature's way of compensating them for when game was difficult to find and kill. On feasting occasions it was said that a member of a San tribe could eat enough at one sitting to fill a lion and all the excess fat went to the buttocks as a reserve food store. They are like the Australian aboriginals, natural and superb trackers and hunters who know every place possible to find water, even if just in a plant. Their language is peculiar because it is a series of 'clicks' and must be one of the most difficult to learn in the whole world. They were brutally slaughtered in the past, treated as nothing but two legged animals to be shot and killed for sport but now some have been assimilated into modern living. They are still inclined to be wary of whites and even some black people but who can blame them with their horrendous history.

We drove into the reserve and our guide and driver took us to see a remarkable plant, a euphorbia which can grow to the height of two men. It has poison so deadly there is no known antidote; the smallest scratch means death. We were also shown a tree called the *kokerboom*, an aloe known as 'the quiver tree' because the Bushmen use it for the quivers to hold their arrows tipped with the deadly poison.

Another remarkable plant was the *welwitschia,* which is strictly protected and considered one of the world's oldest plants. There is a prize specimen whose location is kept very secret and only shown to *bone fide* botanists. The plant we were shown was very tiny indeed, probably only about 12 inches, but it had been calculated it was 1500 years of age. The one whose locality was kept such a dark and deadly secret had been a youngster before Christ was born.

We were also told that living in this area was a species of antelope quite capable of going two weeks without water. Its bodily functions had changed so much that it simply recycled its own urine as a survival tactic.

All these fascinating details are that which one learns when a guide is engaged. Well worth every penny.

We spent two days in this game park living in very comfortable cabins and eating in a communal dining room. Each day we went out in land rover to view the wild animals as they went about their daily lives. Unfortunately we did not see any of the big cats but there was a herd of wild elephant and our drivers kept our vehicles at a very prudent distance. The matriarch of the herd kept her eyes on us and a couple of times slapped her ears in warning. There was no bull around. It was a herd of females with their young and they all did exactly as the matriarch dictated. Their discipline was instinctive and rather impressive.

In the evening we attended open-air barbecues, which were great fun and were impressed by the clear skies that encouraged the construction of a very fine observatory. Many of the trees looked odd because their tops were flattened as if someone had sat on them. This was another wonderful experience for us to enjoy together but it was only a short stay because we were due to fly back down to Cape Town and explore Table Mountain.

And what a mountain it is too. We were incredibly lucky because there were no clouds, which often shroud the mountain. The locals say "she has her tablecloth on", a most charming and appropriate description. We were advised to visit the top of the mountain before she put her tablecloth back on again, which is what we did. We went up by cable car and spent a few hours on the mountaintop, where the views are out of this world.

We were lucky because the next day the tablecloth was back once more. It would have been a rotten day to go up so instead we took a coach trip to Cape Point. This position is a headland not as highly elevated as the mountain but it did enable us to see the two oceans. The Atlantic and Indian oceans meet at this point and it was obvious that they didn't always agree because there was quite a swell where the waters tried to overlap each other.

On the way back in the coach we saw a lot of baboons around. I don't care for any of the monkey family and the only thing that impressed me about these were the vicious fangs they displayed at us. They were not joking either.

The next day was another coach trip through Stellenbosch and we also saw Groot Constantia. From Cape Town we went up the coast to Durban, homeland of the mighty Zulus. I had read a lot about Chaka and Cetewayo and the Zulus in general. This tour was interesting because we passed Spion Kop to one side and thought of the Boer war and all the men, on both sides, who died on that mountainside. We were not all that far from Rourke's Drift, scene of another great battle in the Zulu War, where so many Welsh soldiers earned Victoria Crosses.

We went out to the Drackensburg Mountains and once more the weather was kind to us. While Roy sunbathed I joined a group to go riding, and what fun that was, although the saddle was very uncomfortable.

Our final stop was to be at Johannesburg and to go down a goldmine. How evocative is the word 'gold'. As I had been down a coalmine in Britain I was particularly interested to observe a goldmine. The world's deepest mines are in this area, where men work at the depth of about 4,000 metres. Even with modern technology they could not go much deeper because of the heat. What I found of particular interest was that the shaft, for descent, had to be in three sections. It was quite out of the question to drill a shaft and keep it vitally straight to that depth. What they did was to drill the first shaft to a set landing, then another and if necessary a third. That was how they coped with trying to go so deep. Men and equipment had to go down in three separate stages.

We stepped out of the cage on the first landing and my hair probably stood on end with horror. I swear it lifted off my helmet. There was a very large miner holding a candle – with a naked flame! This was against everything that had been brainwashed into me by my Yorkshire family. Naked flames and mines simply did not go together.

Our guide saw the expression on my face and I hastily explained my Yorkshire heritage and upbringing. He grinned and said there was no gas at all in this part of the pit. 'That's as maybe,' I thought. 'But I still don't like to see a naked flame underground.

Contrary to popular belief, gold is rarely found in yellow veins nowadays. That day's output would come from very tiny specks and it would take 1 ton of ore to produce a mere 8 grams of gold. In the early days, in many countries in the world, gold was found in prominent veins but those have long since been worked out.

When this part of the tour was completed, and very interesting it was as well, we were taken to a large room in which was a table on which were gold bars. Everyone was invited forward and told if they could lift one bar above their head with one hand it would be theirs. The value at the time for each bar was £210,000 Sterling. There were some strong men present and they all pounded up to try their luck to no avail. That offer had not been made for nothing. So I went up. I wanted to see if I could move it at all. I had heard so much about the weight of this metal. That bar weighed 56 Imperial pounds and was still only 80% gold. I flexed my strong arm muscles, gripped with both hands and moved it from one side for a fraction of an inch. Never before or since had my hands been around so much money, though it didn't do me a bit of good. It was another unique experience which was what we both liked, especially myself.

Then we were home again and once more I flung myself into my writing. I had copious notes, seemingly a Table Mountain of them, some written in pencil, others in biro, all collected over many long months of research at the library. I had an idea what I wanted to say and the respective characters had begun to flesh themselves out, so I started typing. We had obtained a more modern machine but it was still a manual and was hard work, which went on for month after weary month. When I had everything down on paper it was a pile of paper a good 4 inches thick.

It was not a book, of course, but ideas for a number of them. Gradually these would have to be broken down but what I was doing now was simply gathering it all together. I knew there was still an awfully long way to go.

We began to talk about having a little break away in between our long overseas holidays. We had been to the Isles of

Man and Anglesey but the Channel Islands were unknown territory so we plumped for Guernsey. I had no idea what would eventually come from this trip. In due course we visited all the other Channel Islands, Jersey, Alderney, Sark and Herm.

Roy liked Jersey best but I preferred Guernsey. On the latter island I was a visitor made enormously welcome by everyone, everywhere. On Jersey I was a tourist with money and with all the connotations attached to money. Sorry people of Jersey, but that's how you made me feel.

We were totally ignorant but went out of our way to investigate and learn that although they were part of the British Isles they were most certainly not part of the United Kingdom or the European Union. Furthermore neither did the writ of Westminster run there. They had their own bailiff, their own Boss Man, and when their Parliament called the States was sitting, the UK representative, the Governor, had to sit on a seat lower down than the bailiff. This was to drive home the point they were very independent.

We also learned, somewhat to our amusement initially, that they most certainly did not belong to England. As William the first, the Duke of Normandy went to Guernsey first before he conquered England; they consider England belongs to them. They are not joking either. It can be quite a touchy subject. Furthermore when the monarch does visit them it is not as king or queen but Duke of Normandy first and monarch very much second.

They also had a system called *The Haro*, which was unique to them. If a person felt dreadfully wronged all they did was collect a witness and call out "*Haro, Haro, Haro! A mon aide, mon prince! Il me fait tort*" then recite the Lord's prayer in French. This simple action had the force of an immediate injunction when the matter had to go to the courts for their decision and remedy. We were both rather impressed with this because such action certainly saved a lot of violent rows in a dispute. Perhaps it should be brought over here!

We thoroughly explored the island then went over to Herm on the short launch crossing and stamped all around there on two visits. Shell beach was most fascinating because we were told that many of the little periwinkle shells had been washed from South America and travelled right across the Atlantic. When wet some were quite beautiful with their lovely colours but were inclined to lose this when dry.

When we came home, quite by chance I picked up the *Daily Mail* newspaper. We always took the *Western Daily Press*. Inside the *Mail* were a few columns on Guernsey. Under the Freedom of Information Act certain files had been released for public disclosure but, and this was the crunch bit as far as I was concerned, seven files had been withheld under the 100 years rule. Now that is a very long time indeed to keep information secret, especially when it related to a little island. All this had been done at the instigation of one of our MPs.

I told Roy I wanted to go there again and start asking questions because I was very curious indeed. He warned me that it was unlikely I would get answers when something was so drastic the 100 years rule applied.

We had already decided upon our next long overseas holiday, which was to be South America, particularly the Amazon jungle from the Brazilian side but the Channel Islands were so near and the living accommodation so reasonable we would have no more problem going there than up to Yorkshire. I had already bought and read *The Book of Ebenezer le Page* by G.D. Edwards, which I had thoroughly enjoyed; it was written using Guernsey colloquial language.

With regard to our forthcoming trip to Brazil, we were told we must take special medical precautions as we had planned to go into the jungle. Anti-malaria tablets were to be taken for number of weeks before we went off to Brazil and also upon our return. At the same time, once we arrived in the country, we must take extra tablets so we dutifully stocked up and took note of what we were told. Then our GP told us we must have yellow fever injections. He could not give these to us. We would have to go to a special place in Bristol which of course we did. We had the address, found the building and went swanning in to find we had come through the wrong door and were at the VD clinic. We simply fell about laughing at this and such amusement surely meant it was going to be a good holiday. We were to find out.

We flew down to South America but had to stop to refuel at Recife. As it was only a very short refuelling stop we were not allowed off the plane and by the time we arrived at Río de Janeiro we were washed out. It was worse for Roy than for me because he was such a huge man, crammed into a little seat. We could not afford to travel business class but only, as Roy described it, 'cattle class'.

It took us a good 24-hours to recover and as this was another touring holiday we just had a short time in Rio on this leg of the journey. Our next main stop was at Brasília, a purpose-built new capital carved from the jungle in the shape of an aeroplane. The wings made the residential areas while the fuselage was for administration. All the architecture was ultramodern, which a person either loves or loathes, there is nothing in between.

What did attract us was a Catholic church of contemporary design, one of the walls of which was made from nothing but blue glass which ranged from the deepest shade to the most delicately pale. The various blues were broken here and there with tiny speckles of white and effect of the whole was quite outstandingly beautiful. It certainly was the highlight of the capital to us.

We went to Manaus in the heart of the jungle, a region of legends and the mystery of Colonel Fawcett's disappearance in the early part of the 20th century. Jungle – what an evocative word. As usual we hired a guide and this became another memorable experience. A group of us were carefully shepherded and this day's memories rank with the eruption of Stromboli and the great Australian Barrier Reef.

A jungle becomes an alien world when one steps onto an animal trail. Long foliage must be brushed aside and a person sweats almost to death. A living jungle has a particular smell with strange sounds, none of which we could identify of course. We plodded along behind our guide to the banks of the River Negro where a launch awaited and now we really understood the river's name. It is truly black, with white froth only at the sides. 'Not unlike Guinness', Roy commented. We cruised down the river to where it widened enough for a huge raft to float. On this a good lunch had been prepared then we were invited to pop into the river for a swim. I went a bit rigid and some of us asked questions about alligators and piranha fish. The guide explained that neither of the two lived on this stretch of the river so a number of us plunged in. It was like swimming in a hot bath and I was not at all enthusiastic. I soon came out, much to Roy's relief.

Later I allowed myself to be taken on a little canoe trip, so I could watch the wildlife from a closer perspective. Roy knew he was much too large so he sat and watched us with a cold beer provided from a portable refrigerator.

We hadn't gone half a dozen strokes when a pair of very ugly eyes rose above the waterline on top of a head which must have been all of two feet long. I gulped and pointed and determined to have a word with guide when we returned, which I did, whereupon he became very quiet and sheepish. Stupid man. No alligators indeed!

The next day's excursion was equally astounding and much safer. Again it was by launch and the air was thick with humidity. We gently motored down the river, which was now the Amazon and came to another of the world's wonders. At this point, and for many miles afterwards, the Amazon and the Negro rivers flow in the same channel but do not mix at all. There was a distinct line, as if drawn by a pen, in which the two waters flowed together, black and brown, and kept rigid side-by-side formation. It was explained to us this was caused by the different soils and chemicals through which the rivers ran. When they meet it is a physical impossibility for them to merge. This peculiar act of nature is called *The Wedding of the Waters* and is certainly something to see.

The last day at Manaus was to visit their stunning opera house. Manaus itself is deep enough to take quite large liners as it is navigable from the ocean 1,000 miles away. Many of the buildings are ramshackle affairs and it seemed incongruous to have an opera house in such a setting. It was all the work of the rich rubber barons, who had so much money they didn't quite know what to do with it all. They had the opera house built and paid for divas to come out from Europe to entertain them, which they did. These fantastically rich men demanded they have their culture. The opera house itself was imported, lock, stock and barrel from Europe. The opera singers soon followed. The rubber monopoly was finally broken by a Briton stealing rubber seeds to plant elsewhere in the empire but despite this the opera house is kept in tiptop condition. It is a complete credit to the Brazilians.

The climate, however, is quite atrocious to those not born there because, with the high humidity, everything is so wet. We expected something different when we went down to São Paulo. It was indeed different but not as we thought. As we were crossing a busy road, on an official crossing and with the lights, Roy was mugged and his wallet was stolen by a pair of thieves. One barged into him on the crossing to distract him while the other dived into a pocket to extract the wallet. It was all done very quickly. We were dreadfully shocked and reported it to the police, not that we expected any action. We also told our guide.

Fortunately, we always made a point of having two signatures on our travellers' cheques and I acted as banker. I kept the bulk of the money in a body belt next to my skin, under a loose top. Roy did go back to see if he could spot the thieves but they were young, agile and long gone. This rather put a shadow on the rest of our time in that country.

Nevertheless, we had a schedule to keep to, for which we had paid, so we flew down to Iguacu, which is on the border between Brazil and Argentina. The waterfalls here are two miles wide. When Eleanor Roosevelt visited she commented that in comparison Niagara Falls was nothing but a faucet.

As we walked down the path, studying this mighty spectacle, everywhere was filled with giant tropical butterflies which were all the colours under the sun. We were still despondent at losing what was, to us, quite a large amount of money and something had to be done. I telephoned London to report the theft to our insurers and was promptly told that because we were in a dollar zone we must report it to New York. Those phone calls cost an arm and a leg but we were bound to make them under the terms of our insurance.

We came back to Río still feeling despondent but our spirits suddenly lifted. The Brazilian tourist board had heard about what had happened to an ageing British couple and, as we were in a day early, they put us in another hotel. At that time in this country all hotel tariffs were displayed on the back of the bathroom door. We were shocked when we were ushered into a large and luxurious suite. Roy took one look at the tariff and went straight down to reception to tell them that we did not have that kind of money but it was explained to us that it was a gift from the country as a token of apology for what had happened to us. What kindness! This gesture lifted our spirits and we strutted around this suite, which was enormous, with multiple rooms and a private balcony. Later on we were told that whenever the late Frank Sinatra came here this was his suite and his alone, so for one 24-hour period in my life I have lived the life of the rich and famous. Even our meals were free.

We only had a short time left in Río, so went on a coach trip to the top of the mountain where the famous statue of Christ overlooks the city. It must have been very difficult to construct and erect. From just about all over Rio one can see this statue, its position is so dominant.

Then, once again, we were heading back home to our flat and to collect our cats from the cattery. We were no longer in the first flush of youth and realized it might be questionable how much longer we could go on doing this, while the money lasted, so for the next year we decided it would be America and Canada on a Greyhound coach.

Guernsey was also on my agenda and as soon as we could we were over there again and I started chatting to people. I picked those of my own age group, the generation who went through the war. I also scoured the two very good libraries at St Peter Port. Very gradually I began to have ideas about those mysterious seven files but because I could not obtain one single fact my supposition has always been kept to myself, even today.

From my enormous of typed work I extracted two books and wrote *Republic* and *Bold Spirit,* then started on the dreary business of approaching publishers. When a work does not come from an agent publishers are inclined to sling a typescript on the slush pile to read some time. This means many months can go by before the writer has any kind of response.

It was a long time since I had been published in fiction, the last book being *Land and Power* with Robert Hale. Also I realised that there had been a change in the publishing world and not necessarily for the better. The Internet was to blame.

At the same time I had started the book on Guernsey, which really fascinated me. My characters were alive I could see and feel them. I had worked out my storyline so all I had to do was write the book and sell it. So simple to type these words but a mighty task in itself, but I can be as obdurate as my late father when the mood strikes me.

I had also been extremely cheeky and sent some features to three in local newspapers. Two of the editors called me up for interview and engaged me as a freelance for more features. One wanted anything of a historical nature on any subject of my choosing while a second simply wanted features about places in the region where he sold.

So I became pretty well occupied, which suited me down to the ground. I had enormous pleasure when my features came out in the various newspapers and I went back to using the name of Wallis Peel. H M Peel had been that used on the children's books and I wished to have differentiation.

Chapter XV

Our trip to North America commenced by flying into Kennedy Airport in New York where we had to change planes for a domestic flight to the West Coast, where we landed at Los Angeles. Within five minutes of leaving the airport on the way to the pre-booked hotel something struck me. Wheels! All the vehicle wheels were so clean and shiny that they sparkled as if made from jewels.

Americans are a very generous and friendly people and very liberal with their meals although their waste is profligate, which horrified us. People would order a meal, eat just a little then leave the rest to be thrown away; and they piled their plates mountain high. We also found their food just a little too sweet for our palates, even white bread and mom's famous apple pie we didn't care for at all for this very reason.

Their hotels are not bed and breakfast like ours. A person simply hires the room and pays extra to eat in the dining room. We rarely used these. We kept our eyes open and followed the habits of the locals by going to diners. Here the food was always excellent and at a very reasonable price, although we thought there was a huge lack of fresh green vegetables and ended up craving sprouts, cauliflower and even cabbage. Americans always serve a side dish of salad with everything but I don't regard these as 'greens'.

We found great insularity with their media, especially concerning Europe. We disapproved of this. As Huxley said: "no man is an island unto himself". Very true indeed. Once it was obvious we were both foreign and British up would come some American. "Hi you Brits!" would be their normal very friendly greeting. "Where are you from? Where are you going? What you think of the States?" Their questions would tumble out but they were all so friendly and meant no harm at all. I wonder what it is like now after the horrors of 9/11? If anything good did come out of that dreadful business it may be that it removed American insularity, especially with the events of Iraq, Afghanistan and the Middle East in general.

Our tour included a trip to Calico, which is a ghost town, quite high up in the mountains under a baking sun, where the colour spectrum is restricted to browns, fawns and greys. This was a silver mining town whose history has been recreated as a tourist attraction. Sheriff Duffy met our coach, wearing genuine six-shooters and spare bullets lodged in his belt. I noticed three gaps among the bullets and itched to ask where they had gone. Had Jesse James suddenly returned? It was all rather comical and very light-hearted.

From Calico we went to Las Vegas, where our hotel was on the famous Strip. What a place this is! At night the coloured lights rival half a dozen Blackpools, dazzling to our eyes and bemusing to our senses, as were the casinos. Inside these there are neither clocks nor windows, no way to tell night from day. The idea is to keep people gambling upon a multitude of machines or at the green and baize tables, all of which had lovely young female croupiers.

I had never played a slot machine in my life but I simply had to have a go right now. Very carefully I fed a humble quarter (25 cent piece) into the machine. To my astonishment it started to make a peculiar noise and suddenly a large silver dollar shot out for me. I was tickled pink and decided I would keep it as a souvenir but Roy thought he would like to try so he took it to a dollar machine – and promptly lost it. There was nearly a divorce there and then. That had been *my* silver dollar and he had lost it. Men!

We strolled about the large room, studying the mesmerized faces of the gamblers, hundreds of them in this gambling hall, which was so plush but festooned with armed security men. We admired the dexterity as the croupiers handled the cards and dealt them. I would have had them all over the floor.

Our bedroom was enormous and I swear that there could have held half a dozen people. I awoke early the next morning at 5.30 and out of animal curiosity went down to the gambling hall again. I was astonished and also felt pity. I recognized many faces from the previous evening. They had been there all night, gambling non-stop. As bad a drug as heroin can ever be.

Our coach next day meandered over the Hoover Dam, which was quite interesting but not to us after what we had seen in Siberia, which we tactfully kept to ourselves! We arrived at the Grand Canyon and what can I say that has not already been said? It is a vertical mile deep with a Native American village at the bottom. The colours, the rock formations and the sheer depth are mind-boggling. The total immensity of this canyon has to be seen to be believed.

After this we were taken to Zion Canyon with a horrendous switchback road from top to bottom. The interesting point here is the rocks and mountains are scarred and gouged from the last Ice Age. The final Canyon we saw became our favourite and this was Bryce. Strictly speaking this is not a true canyon because it does not have two sides which fall away. On one side there is a plain. What it does have though is the most astounding colours which range from reds and pinks through yellows and oranges to fawns and whites. The rocks themselves have been carved into weird, jagged shapes from wind and weather.

Our next stop was at Salt Lake City which was built by and is the spiritual home of the Church of Jesus Christ of Latter-day Saints, otherwise known as the Mormons. It is a delightful, beautifully planned place, spotlessly clean and I disliked it instantly. It was all just too good to be true. This statement is no reflection on the rights or wrongs of this religion. It was simply not my taste and smacked of artificiality.

We headed ever northwards towards Yellowstone Park and Old Faithful. Contrary to popular opinion this geyser does not spout every hour because the times change slightly each year. For us it spouted every 75 minutes and we waited with bated breath, checking our watches and Yes! There she blew! Old Faithful had plenty of competition from boiling mud holes, all of which had an indescribable stench, with the mud bubbling and belching in a quite disgusting manner, sometimes even being thrown into the air in a weird, macabre dance. These holes were laden with chemicals their edges rimmed with peculiar green colours. Calcium formed in shimmering crystals which sparkled in the sun.

We saw a lot of wildlife: bears, moose, elk and other deer all of which seemed quite unimpressed with our coach. We also saw a large prairie rattlesnake on the road before our coach. A park ranger had to persuade it to move away and said he was astonished to see the snake at this altitude, which was about 6,000 feet, because the nights could get very chilly.

We had an overnight stay at Glacier National Park, where bears are in abundance. Our tour guide gave us a very serious warning and lecture about these dangerous animals. Bears can move at an incredible speed, certainly a lot faster than humans, and they are quite good at tree climbing. If we wanted to wander around, the safest way was to make a lot of noise, singing, whistling or ringing a little bell, which was provided for us. The noise would make bears shy away, so we faithfully did as we were told.

From here we crossed into Canada where there were many Native Americans from various tribes, the largest of which were the Navajo. The land we were now on belonged to the Blackfoot reservation and we were highly amused by one sign outside a shop run by them. It said quite simply but to the point, FRIENDLY INDIANS!

The majesty and grandeur of the Rocky Mountains in Canada are breathtaking and some of the highest, most spectacular peaks, had glaciers. Many of these peaks were also still snow-capped, jagged and menacing in their beauty. We shortly left the Indian lands and moved into that of the Inuit, otherwise known as Eskimos.

We fell in love with Canada and her wild beauty. We headed for Vancouver and became fascinated with tall Indian totem poles that had the most remarkable carvings which turned them into genuine works of art. We explored and walked as far as we could in the time available before we boarded our coach again to turn around and start the southward journey.

We passed Mount St Helens, which had exploded with such devastating effect a few years ago. We went through Seattle, Portland and Eureka as we headed back to California. There was one remarkable show yet to come as we entered a forest of the giant redwood trees, the incomparable *Sequoia Sempervirens*. These trees have such incredible height, solidity and girth that tunnels have been cut into their trunks through which cars can drive quite easily. It has been calculated a few were 200 years old when Christ was born and one was so tall it was longer than a football field.

Then we arrived at San Francisco and had just two days there. It was tremendous just going around the city to be fascinated by their trams with their famous clang-clang as they went up and down the switchback roads. We went and had lunch at Fishermen's Wharf, which bristled with shops, restaurants, street entertainers, artists and lovely gardens. There were many trips available including over to Alcatraz, the infamous prison made famous by the film *The Bird Man of Alcatraz*, the nemesis also of Al Capone.

We elected to go around the submarine the USS *Pampanito* instead. This was another experience and made us both realize that submariners are a definite breed apart from all other sailors. Those cramped quarters, the limited headroom and the fact of being shut in what often became a metal tomb.

We took a little coach ride around and were taken to the San Andreas fault and it was a bit spooky to get out of the coach and stand on it. It was explained to us that all the buildings now must be constructed of steel which, theoretically, will merely bend and whip. In our hotel room I happened to look in the phone book and right at the beginning, in a most prominent position, were instructions what to do in the event of an earthquake. It said quite clearly that one of the safest places in a building was to open the door and stand surrounded by the door frame. This would never have occurred to us.

The final drive back to Los Angeles was alongside the Pacific coastline, parts of which are not unlike Cornwall except on a much larger scale. We passed the homes of the wealthy, including that of Randolph Hearst, which puzzled me. Why, with all his wealth, did he elect to build so near to such a hazardous earthquake fault?

Our final two days were spent at Disneyland Anaheim, where we became just another couple of big kids having tremendous fun. It had been an astounding if exhausting tour and the Americans had done us proud.

Upon our return I contacted an agent with my Guernsey book. It was by now 140,000 words long. I was told it needed completely rewriting and the person would then try. Back to the typewriter again and then I then had the work put on disk by someone with a computer. Once more up to London and the matter was in the agent's hands.

The other written works were put to one side and then I lost my freelance newspaper writing. It was not my copy but a sign of the times. There was the Enron scandal, the pensions' debacle plus the general economic climate. The newspaper groups had started to lose advertising revenue because of eBay and were being forced to cut down drastically. All freelancers had to go. I even knew one top-notch press photographer who was also made redundant. He promptly set up as self-employed and is doing all right.

At the same time there was a general uproar in two large newspapers which I know but who will remain nameless. Long-standing, reputable and well thought of editors departed from these two good papers on one hour's notice. This was utterly shocking. What on earth was going on? The next thing I heard was that the reporters of another paper had all marched outside and held a union meeting on the pavement. Not that it did them any good. The newspaper world in general appeared to be in one almighty mess.

They were not alone either. Many of the literary agents were finding it difficult and sometimes almost impossible to place a typescript with a publisher. The agent who I was using was also having problems. The agent's income depends upon the percentage agreed to come from the author's royalties. No book sales through them simply meant no income. Those based in London had very expensive rates to pay before they considered their utility bills and possible profit. The whole book world seemed to be in an insane mess and it boded no good to me. I started to become very uneasy indeed with justification. At the end of a number of months the agent sent my book back. She had tried but to no avail. It was just another sign of those years.

I was disappointed, of course, but who else to try? Although I had a track record it was a long time since I had been published and I was never exactly famous – or notorious! I had nothing specific which I could show to sell myself so for the time being I did exactly nothing.

At the same time we were heading towards pensionable age and what the future held we had no idea. Roy suggested we have one more big holiday and call it a day because of our age and limited finances. I wasn't too sure what he had in mind because I'm no great lover of ships. I get seasick and the fact Nelson used to get seasick too cuts no ice with me. He suggested a cruise up to the Arctic, which would certainly be different from the norm of cruising for sunshine, so that was what we decided.

We opted to go on a Soviet cruise liner because they have a very good reputation and down at Tilbury we boarded the liner. As it was to be our last proper holiday Roy had booked a suite, albeit a very small one. The only snag was that it was in the bows of the ship and I was not at all certain how my stomach would react if we had bad weather!

Our first port of call was Amsterdam in the Netherlands. This brought back memories of when I hitchhiked around as a young single girl with hardly two pennies to my name. It was all very nostalgic but unfortunately there was not time to hire a car, go over the Zuider Zee and look at the farmhouse I had stayed at. Ships and tides wait for no man!

The next place we visited was the Faroes – and what a bleak, treeless place this is. There are many houses and churches there which have their roofs grassed over, a very practical way to insulate; grass sods are hardly likely to blow off in a gale, unlike slate tiles. We toured the capital, Torshaven, and learned that these islands belonged to the Danes. Quite frankly, they're welcome to them. Even in the summer we found the climate bleak, wet and cold.

From here we went to Iceland, a country I had always wanted to visit. Roy knew this and it was his bait to get me to agree to another cruise! Oh, the cunning of men!

We followed our usual custom of obtaining a guide and coach to take a tour so we could get maximum viewing. It seemed strange to see geysers and hot water pools like those at Yellowstone. This is another almost treeless country but by the side of a waterfall I was shown a fully grown tree. It was just about 24 inches tall!

This country has abundant thermal energy that has been tapped to provide heat and hot water. We also spotted the most astonishing greenhouses, all heated by thermal power, with plants and flowers which would put Kew Gardens to shame. Many of their volcanoes are considered extinct but I use this word circumspectly. At one stage on this tour our coach went across the lava flow of a supposedly dead volcano. The driver did not bat an eyelid but we were quite delighted to get back on terra firma again.

We sailed again and it took us three days to reach Spitsbergen in the Arctic, which belongs to Norway under an international treaty, although it had a large contingent of Soviet miners. It may also be remembered we British had a military raid against these coal mines during World War II which was a similar failure to that at Dieppe, probably due to counterintelligence from a German spy.

We arrived in the early hours and when I opened the bedroom curtains I gasped with surprise. The liner had anchored at the foot of deep, snow-clad mountains and on one side was a glacier. We dressed quickly and when topside to find air that was very cold but also dry.

The Russians made perfect hosts. They have a great knack to make a simple visit memorable and on that day they surpassed themselves. The crew were landing that morning and then we passengers went ashore by launch. We were astounded when we scrambled ashore into quite deep snow. A host of deckchairs had been carefully erected and placed firmly in the snow. There were numerous portable toilets and a barbecue was in full swing with a real feast. There was even a Polar Bear bar! I have done some strange things in my life but this one really took the biscuit. There we were, muffled against the cold, sitting in deckchairs with snow up to our knees – having a really good picnic! It was hilarious! It was also enormous fun and the food was out of this world. Then we were at liberty to walk around in the snow and view everything – including a few old graves.

There was a loud noise as a helicopter appeared and landed. Out stepped two gigantic Norwegian policemen. They had come to make sure we were all behaving ourselves on their island and that we did not leave one piece of litter or cigarette butt behind.

After we had all been ferried back to the liner in boats, the Russians cleaned up with scrupulous care. All that was indeed left behind were our footprints. Everywhere else bristled with cleanliness.

We turned to sail south in Norway and underwent a very rare experience, so unusual that even the Russians who were off duty rushed up to watch with their cameras. We passengers ignored meals to view the rare scene which unfolded before us. We had sailed into a gigantic ice field. The Russian captain took us through it and never left the bridge. There were many times when his experienced eyes warned him, the engines would go into reverse and the liner would sail around some particularly thick ice. We were told by some of the officers that such an ice field, at this time of the year, was totally unexpected. With so many civilian passengers on board the liner would not have come if it had been known about. After all, has anyone forgotten the Titanic?

We finally reached Honnigavaag in Norway in the evening and more coaches awaited to take us up to North Cape to see the full sun at midnight. A wind had arisen which came straight down from the North Pole with tremendous velocity. Each breath seemed to sear the lungs and our nostrils bled.

This was all incredibly new. We had to breathe into a scarf to protect our lungs. There was a railing and I hauled myself along then I was there! I stood at the top of North Cape and defied the elements. It was just past midnight and the sun shone down, all yellow but so bitterly cold.

I turned to retrace my steps when the wind gusted even more strongly. It actually lifted me off my feet for quite a few inches, which was very eerie. Then it plopped me back down again, still vertical. It was so uncanny I tried an experiment. I turned and leaned right forward with my body stiff and did not fall. The wind kept me erect, supporting the whole of my body weight. Now that was really something.

From North Cape we sailed through the outer coastal fjords to Tromso. This place is very proud of its polar cathedral, the most northerly in the world. The architecture pleased our eyes, as did the backdrop of mountains. This is the home of the Laplanders and we saw many dressed in their national costume, which is quite charming, but we did not spot Father Christmas as it was off-season for him!

Our last port of call was at Stavanger, further south. Then we headed into the North Sea and home. It had been the most remarkable experience thanks to the care and efficiency of the Russian officers and crew. The food they gave us was out of this world and always set out in beautiful patterns. We even had the luxury dish of sturgeon from the Volga, which was most delicious. Nothing was too much trouble for these lovely people.

Now two old age pensioners were to settle down at home, having seen and done just about everything of note.

Chapter XVI

The first thing we did was acknowledge that we should get out of our flat because there were 21 stairs leading to it and we were becoming a little bit decrepit. We obtained a pensioner's bungalow and, along with our sole feline pet, Katy, we moved. It would be the last move of our life so we took the opportunity to have a grand clear out. Over the years we had acquired a bit of antique furniture which was delightful but weighed a ton. That went first of all, then we went through every room and ruthlessly removed everything that we would not want in the future. It was quite amazing what we had acquired throughout our marriage. It was useful work because when we moved into our new bungalow we still had what was essential but were not cluttered up with superfluous objects.

I had ground to a halt with my writing. I had tired myself out sending work out but it all came bouncing back with demoralizing regularity and I did not quite know what to do for the best. There was no newspaper writing either, which was a shame, but I decided that all the features I had written in the past about Gloucestershire would one day come out in a non-fiction book.

I started to have trouble with my neck and spine, which required surgery. It never entered my head what was to come later. I am a person who refuses to know the future.

Roy was five years older than me and suddenly became an old man. We were both so thankful we had spent the last few years travelling. We would never go anywhere again but neither could anyone steal our memories. We often sat and reminisced about the places we had been and the sights we had seen.

Prior to this retirement and in between our long foreign holidays, I had gone to Prague on a number of visits and met my pen-pal Alexandra. We had wonderful times together and she came over here twice. She had a yearning to see Land's End, which I suppose is understandable coming from a landlocked country. And she saw it.

During our multitude of conversations on numerous visits we discovered an unusual fact. Her father's surname was Bulin, which is neither a Czech nor a German name. Very slowly we worked it out that some distant ancestor of hers was from the Bullen family and must have come over to this part of Europe. It may have been because of religious persecution or political troubles but it was quite impossible to find out because so many documents had been destroyed in World War II. We concluded that there was a reasonable possibility that we were distant cousins.

I was over there when the Berlin Wall came down and what sights we both saw with the East Germans fleeing into West Germany in tiny, polluting cars which were mostly little boxes on four bits of rubber. This also became the start of today's Czech Republic and I was glad I was there to see the country obtain its freedom and become democratic.

Alex, though, was not at all healthy. She had hepatitis C and in 2003 she died. I had lost my adopted sister. It was all very sad because we had exchanged letters for over half a century but I was just so thankful we were able to enjoy holidays together here, in the Czech Republic and also Poland, where we went on a trip.

Everything bad has to end but so does everything good. Alexandra died in March 2003 and Roy started to become unwell in July that same year. The doctor thought it might be a form of bronchitis but Roy refused to go into hospital initially. Then, after three weeks sitting in his chair, he agreed. I called the doctors out one Sunday morning and within half an hour he was in hospital. Nine days later, he was dead.

I just could not believe it. I could not take it in. It was just three months from our golden wedding and I nearly went off my trolley with grief and despair. I did not know what had killed him and demanded an immediate post-mortem. As it happened, the hospital doctor refused to sign his death certificate so there had to be a coroner's post-mortem and inquest. It was revealed that Roy had died from mesothelioma, caused by exposure to asbestos during his wartime Royal Naval service 60 years earlier. It had started to peak in men of his generation. There is no cure whatsoever.

The weeks that followed have become impossible to remember, except that our little pet Katy kept me going. She was getting old and would never have been re-homed, so I had to carry on for her, no matter my distress.

Roy and I had been so long together and done so much as a couple that my world had quite collapsed around me. As mentioned before, we never had children for some reason but I did have a small circle of genuine, sincere and very caring friends. They say one is lumbered with family and close friends are chosen. I knew I was very lucky.

Even though Roy died testate the legal formalities with a death can be quite horrendous. I found this out with one savings account, which was with Northern Rock of all places. I had a solicitor dealing with them and they proved to be the most awkward people imaginable. They refused to answer letters, were never available on the telephone and in the end the solicitor rang almost in despair. I took over. I wrote to the financial editor of the *Daily Mail* and told him the whole disgusting story. It was quite amazing. Within two weeks the account was closed and a cheque came to me plus £25 compensation for the problems I had encountered. It was only a few years later when the whole country was up in arms at Northern Rock, so I did well to get out of them what I did – all thanks to the *Daily Mail*.

Nothing happened with my writing because I simply did not know what to do. Nor did I have the heart because a part of me had gone forever through those crematorium doors. The winter came with long dark nights and I was very miserable that first Christmas. Just me and little Katy and there was no telling how long I would have her. She was really starting to age. When she did have to go it would be a final link with Roy broken.

I gave myself a good shaking and started to think. I had joined the Society of Authors in 1960. They are the very strong body who look after the author's interests. They are an independent trade union affiliated to the T.U.C. Every quarter they bring out a magazine and I studied the December issue most carefully. An idea was growing in my brain. I simply had to be mentally occupied. If I couldn't publish commercially, if the agents still rebuffed me, they could all go and get themselves well and truly stuffed. I would self publish, see how it went then endeavour to sell the various other rights myself.

I chose a self-publishing company and contacted the Society of Authors and asked if they could give a reference or any information which could be relevant. Their response was very positive so then I rang the literary consultant whose firm it was. I was quite straight and told her everything. She sent me her contract which I signed and I have been with Jane ever since and I am delighted with what she's done for me. She produces excellent books. Someone whom I knew, in a very large commercial company, paid her the ultimate compliment by saying the books don't look as if they have been self published.

I started off with my Guernsey saga which is based on the island, from all the research I did there, and which covers the period from 1918 to 1945. It is a large book of 140,000 words and I had to have it put on floppy disks. By now I had acquired a computer but I was very much at the novice stage. I had not a shred of confidence with the thing and was horrified at how much there was to learn when I was well into my 70s.

I pressed on though, trying to do exactly as Jane advised. She had the professional nous while I had reverted to being the greenest of learners. My experience to date with producing books had been commercial in which many aspects of the production are the publisher's responsibility. Suddenly I was the publisher and I had to have a name. I chose the name for this town given by the second lot of William the first clerks. Giete. 'Let someone pick the bones out of that,' I muttered to myself. Now that my days and evenings were so fully occupied some of the emotional stress for losing Roy had been pushed to the back of my mind, which was the best place for it, as he would have said.

I won't say it was easy because it was not. Jane was most particular. Every book had to be proofed twice with meticulous detail. There were discussions about the covers and what illustrations. There would also be the running proofs to check from the printers. It was all getting very interesting indeed. I was seeing and experiencing the production of a book, which is often dealt with by the commercial publisher alone.

I sometimes thought back to the old riding days. For one whole winter I had ridden with a local lady who had two horses. When that ended, once a fortnight, I would hire a hack and go for a great two hours' ride. It was enormous fun but Roy was still alive and concerned about my safety. After an operation on my neck I realized I was probably pressing my luck so at 72 years of age I finally hung up my riding boots. It was strange though not to be involved in any way with horses and many a time, when I was going about my domestic duties in the bungalow, I would think back to those days, the fun and tremendous excitement. Even now I have this yearning to sling a leg across a saddle but it would be pretty stupid, to put it mildly. So these were just other memories tucked away in my mental filing cabinet.

I often thought about those early horse adventure books which came out with Harrap. Was a time getting right for republication? This made an interesting thought but again was filed in another mental cabinet drawer. Right now concentration was required to bring out the Guernsey book *Sea Gem*. I had already agreed to go over to the island for signing sessions which would be arranged. This was left to the self-publishing company and the rep we then had.

When the book did come out, with my tongue in my cheek, I sent a copy to be entered in the David St John Thomas awards for self-published books. I was quite thunderstruck when I won the award for that year. It was the first time I had won anything in my life and I felt very chuffed with myself. Can you blame me?

After discussions with the self-publishing company I decided the next one to come out would be all the newspaper features I had written about Gloucestershire. It was non-fiction and I called it *Glorious Gloucestershire*. It was dedicated to my dear friend Carole J Taylor.

I realized it was a little too soon to start trying to move the other rights. It was more important I bring other works out and then go into secondary sales with the greatest vengeance. From starting on the typescript to the finished product took many months of work so I aimed to bring out just one book year and altogether there were half a dozen. These all came from the copious notes and writing which I had done years ago on the manual machine. First though they had to be made suitable through a computer.

Another upset loomed on my horizon which caused me considerable distress. All of a sudden, seemingly within a handful of days, Katy went downhill very rapidly. She was not interested in eating or me and we adored each other. I felt sick at heart, as I knew what I had to do. Just a few days short of 17 years old, one Devon Rex feline had to be taken to the vet for the last time. I stayed with her, talking to her, stroking her little face as the injection went into her leg and she died.

I was in a dreadful state for the rest of the day. I really was totally alone now and it was the breaking of a last link with Roy. I rang up a friend who had connections with the Cats' Protection League and arranged for all her bedding and other articles, plus quite a lot of food, to be collected later that day. I then rearranged the room and was crying buckets the whole time. Katy had kept me going after Roy died and I knew I was now too old to contemplate even a pensioner rescue cat. How I missed that little creature. Only another genuine animal lover will understand these sad sentiments but my life was fated to go on.

So I threw myself back into the world of producing books. The sheer hard work involved was a catharsis because how I missed that little creature. I kept looking for her, listening to her funny little squawk when she demanded something and I could only hope that she was with Roy and the rest of our pets.

I brought out the book *Republic* and then *Bold Spirit* and after that *Spirit of Defiance*, which left just two more books to do. *Battle Royal* was earmarked to appear in 2009 and *Pride of Mercia* in 2010, by which time I would have entered the ranks of the octogenarians. This would also mean all those laborious researched notes of years ago, pre computer days, had been used up. It was a long task but it was good that I had it. I believe it is the Jewish race who warn, "Do not grieve too much or you will be given something even worse." An easy sentence, simple to type out, a true one but hard to obey unless the mind is fully occupied. Mine certainly was now.

At the same time with such a clutch of books out on the shelves I decided now was the time to make other moves. My expenditure was rather high and it seemed appropriate to start to try and turn my affairs in another direction so that perhaps the word profit would appear!

I sent *Bold Spirit* and *Sea Gem* to the BBC Chivers division at Bath for consideration as large print works for libraries. I was delighted when a contract came for the former but disappointed about the latter. The lady who dealt with these matters was taken with the book. She liked it. The problem was the length of 140,000 words, which was simply too much for her imprint. She kept looking at it and calculating but *Sea Gem* in large print would come to 600 pages. To think of taking on a book of this length would obviously blow holes in her budget. With great regret she had to decline but very kindly suggested a place to which I could send it. She warned me not to mention their name because they were competitors to this other publishing house. I sent *Sea Gem* off but knew I would have many weeks to wait because the decisions on accepting a book, and the expenditure they make, has to be carefully considered only after the work has been through a number of readers.

BBC Chivers also eventually send me contracts to bring out in large print *Republic* and *Spirit of Defiance*. In one of my parcels sending book copies to them for consideration, I also included *Land and Power* which came out in 1975 through Robert Hale. To my astonishment and complete delight I received a contract for this book, which totalled four books with the BBC. Naturally, I also let them know when I planned to bring out *Battle Royal* and *Pride of Mercia*. If I don't sell myself, who will?

I sent *Sea Gem* to Isis who produce audio books and received a contract from them as well. They did a splendid job and the book was read by Patience Tomlinson. This was another delight for me and to get money coming in like this was a way to offset the self-publishing expenditure. It was made clear to me that Isis might also be interested in my other books in due course.

Quite by chance I noticed a new small independent publisher had opened in Edinburgh. Their speciality was to bring back to the public children's books no longer printed. I photocopied all of mine and sent them for consideration. There was rather a collection. *Fury* and *Jago* stood alone and then came seven books in my Leysham Stud series, all of which had been written so long ago in the late 50s and 60s and brought out by Harrap. I also included a copy of *The Law of the Wild* which had been read in the year 2000 by Professor David Bellamy. He liked the book and wrote a most delightful foreword for it. The postal costs to get this lot to Edinburgh were out of this world.

The publisher, quite naturally, took a long time to read all of these. They were uncertain about *Fury* and *Jago*, did not like *Law of the Wild* but were attracted to those in the Leysham Stud series. I promptly sent *Law of the Wild* elsewhere for another publisher to read and consider.

At the same time myself and a pal Viv Nichol had worked on and collaborated with a book which we loosely called *Britain A to Z*. It was a non-fiction, educational book aimed at children from about 10 years upwards as well as tourists, who would be curious about our customs and way of life. Then I sent *Glorious Gloucestershire* to another small independent that specialized in coffee table books. I had known all along this latter work required more photographs which I could not afford when I self-published it. I was quite honest and explained all this. The publisher was interested but could not do anything at the moment. Was I prepared to wait? Of course I was! I had been involved in this publishing game for over half a century and I considered I knew how many beans made five. The economic times were harsh in this year with the price of oil leaping through the sky, Middle

East wars to be paid for and the general uproar in the money markets from American sub primes. Domestic living costs were heading towards an astronomical ceiling and, when all was said and done, books were not really essential to basic living. I was quite happy to wait. Softly, softly, catchee monkey has always been true!

Then I decided that, recession or no recession, I would act after all. I brought out *Battle Royal* self-published and also in large print with Chivers. *Pride of Mercia* came out in 2010 and I was confident Chivers would also be interested in this. My large collection of typescripts were all now books, so planned *Birth of The English* for publication in 2011.

I became 80 in 2010. I had gone to pieces, physically, with osteoporosis of the spine and osteoarthritis of both knees but, thank God, my brain was as razor sharp as ever. *Easter The Showjumper* had been republished in 2009 and Magna wanted *Law Of The Wilds* for large print publication in 2010. Other works were elsewhere and I found I was as busy as I had ever been as I approached the 7th anniversary of Roy's death. I was sure he would be pleased with my efforts in my widowhood.

At the same time I collated all my short stories, most of which had not been republished since 1956. They made an interesting read with a linking theme of adventure. I decided they would come out as an anthology for any age group or gender so that joined my 'to do' list after *Birth of the English* had seen the light of day. I also had a large collection of features ranging from the Druids, Monks and witches to the joy of dancing and being with horses. They might be suitable as a coffee table book. All I had to do was keep breathing another handful of years!

When I published *Glorious Gloucestershire* it was with features written for and published in the *Gazette* of Dursley. I completely forgot to insert a bibliography and was told about this by a number of critical readers! Just before my 80th birthday I became dissatisfied because the whole of the Shire was not covered. I decided this was unsatisfactory so wrote appropriate features, which covered Gloucester, in some depth, and shorter ones on Tewkesbury and Cheltenham. The obvious thing left to do then was bring this paperback out again in 2011 with all which I had previously missed. A number of the other features were rewritten and updated, especially that for the powerful River Severn. This river was now the subject of intense interest with feasibility studies concerning harnessing the river's power to make 'green' electricity. Should this be a barrage across the river or a series of lagoons? Either would cost an astronomical amount of money so the decision had to correct. Certainly this book should come out again, extended and updated.

During the course of researching for the historical fiction, I discovered two people whose lives were far from normal which set me thinking. How many more were there like this, people who did not follow the norm through breeding, incidents and temperament? In my quiet periods I decided now was a good time to find what else I could discover and it became a fascinating game. I found 23 English people whose lives, for good or bad, were incredible. Some of them became involved in events so momentous Homo Sapiens was affected for all time. I collected them all into a typescript of 33,500 words and gave the work the title of *They Lived Strange Lives* and sent it to a commercial publisher. This meant I now had something else to sell or self-publish. I simply had to keep breathing a bit longer.

So as I come to the end of this computer work the above is how matters now stand at present. I am quite confident they will improve. At no time in my life have I been prepared to let grass grow under my feet.

~ Fin ~